BRAIN TRAINING
the
JAPANESE
WAY

"It is only through entering the tiger's cave that you are able to catch its cub."

You have to try it in order to make progress.

BRAIN TRAINING
the
JAPANESE WAY

Over 200 Fun and Challenging Puzzles
to **Improve Concentration**,
Strengthen Memory,
and **Boost Brain Health**

Dr. Gareth Moore

Published in the US by
ULYSSES PRESS
P.O. Box 3440
Berkeley, CA 94703
www.ulyssespress.com

First published as *Chiryoku* in Great Britain in 2019 by Pop Press, an imprint of Ebury Publishing Group

ISBN: 978-1-64604-037-7
Library of Congress Control Number: 2020931856

10 9 8 7 6 5 4 3 2 1
Printed in the United States by Kingery Printing

Acquisitions editor: Casie Vogel
Managing editor: Claire Chun
US Proofreaders: Barbara Schultz, Renee Rutledge
Front cover design: Beau Sims

IMPORTANT NOTE TO READERS: This book is independently authored and published and no sponsorship or endorsement of this book by, and no affiliation with, any trademarked brands or other products mentioned or pictured within is claimed or suggested. All trademarks that appear in this book belong to their respective owners and are used here for informational purposes only. The author and publisher encourage readers to patronize the quality brands mentioned in this book.

Contents

Introduction

This book is all about intellectual power. Through a series of 200 puzzles, of 16 elegant Japanese types, you'll have the chance to keep your brain young in the Japanese way.

Your brain loves novelty, and learns best when it is relaxed, so challenging yourself with the variety of fun puzzle content in this book is an excellent way to help look after your gray matter. Not only will you be building your mental skills, but you'll also have the chance to try out a variety of entertaining challenges—and perhaps discover a new favorite puzzle into the bargain.

You'll need a wide range of mental skills to navigate through this book successfully, including mental agility, concentration and number skills, as well as both creative thinking and good observation. Most of all, you'll need to reason logically to make progress.

You'll encounter some puzzle types you may already be familiar with, such as sudoku, but the chances are that the majority of the challenges in this book will be new to you. That's why each type of puzzle starts with an introduction that explains how the puzzle works, and highlights some of the mental skills that learning to solve that puzzle can help develop. There's also a worked example, explaining, step-by-step, how to solve a sample puzzle. It's well worth going through these slowly, to make sure you fully understand the rules of each puzzle.

As you continually challenge your brain with new puzzle varieties, you might find some puzzle types much trickier than others. Don't be tempted to skip over these, however, since these are most likely to be the ones that will bring you the greatest mental benefit. Indeed, there is a Japanese expression: "Fall down seven times, stand up eight." It's good advice.

When you get stuck, don't be afraid to try guessing. You never know what you might discover from the result of your guess, and in a sense it's the purest form of learning. Back when you were a baby you learned to walk by experimenting, using your brain's innate ability to spot patterns and learn through trying. A similar technique will often work with the puzzles in this book, and it's probably the quickest way to become proficient at them. It's certainly not the *only* technique, but it's a good one when you can't see the next deduction to make.

The puzzles are grouped into chapters by area of mental focus, and then within each chapter by puzzle type. In each section, the puzzles start off small to get you into the swing of things, before moving onto several regular-sized challenges. Each section then concludes with a couple of larger puzzles, for tackling once you've mastered the preceding ones.

You can tackle the book in any order you like, but it's best to work through each particular section in the puzzle order given, since they are arranged not just in order of size but also in order of increasing difficulty. You'll also find full solutions at the back, should you want to check your answers—or need a few extra clues on a puzzle.

Good luck, and have fun!

Dr. Gareth Moore
@DrGarethMoore / DrGarethMoore.com

"Learn from your actions,

not from your lessons."

You can read about it all you like,
but you have to give it a go to truly learn.

Mental Agility/Speed

精神的な敏腕

SUDOKU

Unless you've lived under a rock for the past decade, you've probably heard of sudoku. No matter where you go in the world, you will find sudoku magazines and books for sale.

The puzzle's success can be partially explained by its great simplicity. Simply fill the grid so that every number appears once in each row, column, and bold-lined box. There's also something strangely satisfying as you place each number, wresting order from the seeming chaos of the initial numbers.

The puzzles in this chapter, apart from the tutorial opposite, require you to place 1 to 9 once each into every row, column, and bold-lined 3 × 3 box.

Mental Benefits

Sudoku is a purely logical puzzle. There's a single, correct answer, so you will never need to guess to solve the sudoku in this book. It's all about being both methodical *and* thoughtful—not missing the "obvious" deductions, while also spotting the clever inferences that can help you make progress.

Sudoku requires a range of mental skills, since you need to think carefully and rationally about each puzzle, while making progress with sensible, step-by-step moves. This methodical way of thinking is a useful technique for approaching many problems in life.

1.

6		4		2	
			1		
	6				
	1		3		4

- For reasons of space, this puzzle is 6 × 6. To solve it, we need to place numbers so 1 to 6 appear once each in every row, column and bold-lined 3 × 2 box.
- The bottom-left 3 × 2 box must contain a 6, but it can't be in the first or third columns since we already have a 6 in those—so it must be in the middle column.

2.

6		4		2	
			1		
	6				
	6				
	1		3		4

- There is now only one square that a 4 can be placed in in the bottom-left box, since the 4 at the top of the third column and at the right of the bottom row eliminate the other squares.

3.

6		4		2	
			1		
	6				
4	6				
	1		3		4

- Now there is only place for a 3 to fit in the bottom-left box.
- There is also only one place for a 1 to fit in the middle-left box.

4.

6		4		2	
			1		
1		6			
4	6	3			
$\frac{2}{5}$	1	$\frac{2}{5}$	3		4

- The remaining two squares in the bottom-left region must contain a 2 and a 5, in some order. Make a note of this with small pencil marks.
- This means that the only remaining empty square in the bottom row must be a 6.
- The rest of the puzzle can be solved by further, step-by-step observations. For example, perhaps first consider where you can place a 1 in the top-left box.

5.

6	3	4	5	2	1
5	2	1	6	4	3
3	4	2	1	5	6
1	5	6	4	3	2
4	6	3	2	1	5
2	1	5	3	6	4

- The completed puzzle.

Puzzle 1

Puzzle 2

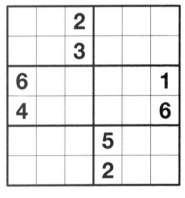

Puzzle 3

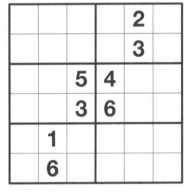

Puzzle 4

BRAIN TRAINING the JAPANESE WAY

Puzzle 5

6		2	1		3	5		8
			9		7			
9		1		6		7		4
7	1			9			8	2
		5	6		8	4		
3	6			1			5	7
5		9		8		3		1
			7		9			
4		7	5		1	8		9

Puzzle 6

		7				9		
	2	9	8		1	3	5	
1	3		7		4		8	2
2				8				5
7	5						3	9
	6	4				2	1	
		2	1		7	8		
			9	5	6			
				4				

Puzzle 7

			3	7	9			
		8		4		7		
	4		2		8		6	
4		3				9		5
6	1						2	7
2		7				6		3
	3		4		2		7	
		4		9		8		
			1	6	3			

Puzzle 8

4		8	9		2	3		6
6	3						7	2
		1	8		7	9		
				2				
		6	5		1	7		
7	6						8	3
8		2	1		6	4		7

BRAIN TRAINING the JAPANESE WAY

Puzzle 9

6								5
	3						2	
5		7				1		9
	8		7		1		5	
4								3
			2		9			
	9			2			1	
			9		4			
		4		6		8		

Puzzle 10

4								8
			9		3			
		3				1		
1	4		2		8		5	3
		7				2		
	3		6		5		9	
2			1		9			4
	8			4			2	

Top grid:

3					7	1		9
	7		5					
		2		6				
	4					3		2
		3				4	6	7
6							9	
9			7	3				
				1	4			
4			2	5				

Bottom grid (overlaps the top grid's lower-right 3×3 block):

				5	9			7
			6	3				
				4	1			8
	3							6
7	4	8				9		
5		9					8	
				2		3		
					6	1		
1		2	3					4

This puzzle has two overlapping grids, which must be solved simultaneously to reach a unique position.

This puzzle has five overlapping grids, including the "hidden" one in the center, which must be solved simultaneously to reach a unique solution.

HITORI

Hitori is, in one sense, the opposite of sudoku, since the aim is to shade and therefore eliminate numbers, rather than add them. Specifically, you must shade numbers so that *no* number appears more than once in any row or column.

Shaded squares cannot touch to the left, right, above, or below. Also, shaded squares must be placed in such a way that all of the remaining *unshaded* squares form a single continuous region. What this means is that you could place your finger on any unshaded square and then trace a path to any other unshaded square without moving over a shaded square or moving diagonally—or lifting your finger.

Mental Benefits

Hitori reverses the fundamental assumptions of sudoku. Because shaded squares cannot touch, if you shade a square then all of the squares around it become definitely unshaded—and you must think about what the implications of this would be. Combined with the need to keep all the white, numbered squares connected, the puzzle can provide a real workout for your reasoning skills.

1.

7	6	7	3	7	4	3
3	6	6	1	7	5	2
5	2	4	4	3	1	6
1	3	7	5	6	2	4
2	4	2	5	2	7	1
6	3	1	5	4	6	7
4	7	5	6	1	2	3

- The middle column has three 5s in succession. The middle 5 can't be shaded because, if it were, it would force there to be two unshaded 5s in that column—right above and right below it. So we know the middle 5 is unshaded, which in turn means that the two surrounding 5s must be shaded.
- Mark definitely unshaded squares with a circle, so you can keep track of your deductions. This includes every square touching a shaded square.

2.

7	6	7	3	7	4	3
3	6	6	1	7	5	2
5	2	4	④	3	1	6
1	3	⑦	5	⑥	2	4
2	4	2	⑤	2	7	1
6	3	①	5	④	6	7
4	7	5	⑥	1	2	3

- You can now shade every repeated number in a row or column that contains that number in a circle.

3.

7	6	7	3	7	4	3
3	6	6	1	7	5	2
5	2	4	④	3	1	6
1	3	⑦	5	⑥	2	4
2	4	2	⑤	2	7	1
6	3	①	5	④	6	7
4	7	5	⑥	1	2	3

- Now you can circle the numbers next to the new shaded squares.
- Continue in this way, remembering that all unshaded squares must be connected, until the puzzle is complete.

4.

7	6	7	3	7	4	3
3	6	6	1	7	5	2
5	2	4	4	3	1	6
1	3	7	5	6	2	4
2	4	2	5	2	7	1
6	3	1	5	4	6	7
4	7	5	6	1	2	3

- The completed puzzle.

Puzzle 1

5	4	5	1	4	3	2
6	6	3	7	2	5	4
2	1	7	3	6	7	6
4	2	6	7	1	5	5
1	3	1	6	4	4	7
4	7	1	2	6	2	5
7	2	5	2	4	2	1

Puzzle 2

5	4	5	6	5	2	7
1	1	2	7	6	4	3
6	7	6	2	6	5	7
3	3	4	1	2	3	5
2	5	7	3	7	1	7
3	2	5	4	1	4	6
7	1	7	5	7	6	4

Puzzle 3

3	2	4	1	1	4	4
1	3	7	2	4	5	6
3	7	1	4	1	3	1
7	3	4	6	3	5	2
4	5	1	2	6	7	7
3	6	3	7	6	1	4
4	1	2	5	7	3	3

Puzzle 4

2	2	3	4	6	4	1
7	5	2	1	2	3	4
6	1	4	1	7	1	3
1	3	2	5	4	7	4
4	7	5	6	3	2	2
5	2	2	3	6	6	4
4	7	6	7	5	2	1

Puzzle 5

1	4	8	2	5	7	7	6
6	6	2	1	7	5	4	8
3	6	2	7	2	2	2	4
8	2	7	1	3	5	6	8
2	5	3	6	4	3	7	1
8	8	1	8	6	8	5	8
8	1	3	5	4	6	7	2
7	2	6	3	8	1	2	5

Puzzle 6

3	6	4	2	5	1	7	1
6	2	8	8	7	3	1	4
3	1	5	8	2	8	6	8
7	8	3	6	6	4	6	2
4	8	1	8	3	8	5	8
8	3	3	1	6	2	6	5
2	5	6	4	1	7	8	7
1	1	7	5	7	6	4	4

Puzzle 7

5	2	7	4	7	8	7	6
7	3	1	3	2	3	8	3
4	7	2	5	8	6	1	2
1	1	5	2	6	7	3	7
6	1	8	7	8	5	4	8
3	2	6	2	4	1	7	1
6	4	8	1	8	7	5	2
8	5	4	2	1	2	6	2

Puzzle 8

6	4	8	7	3	2	3	5
7	2	1	4	1	6	5	1
8	4	3	2	7	5	7	6
1	6	7	6	4	8	2	8
7	4	3	1	2	3	7	6
2	5	4	5	8	1	6	1
5	1	3	3	5	4	7	2
4	8	2	8	6	3	1	3

BRAIN TRAINING the JAPANESE WAY

Puzzle 9

10	9	1	9	6	9	8	9	2	9
3	6	5	2	5	1	5	7	10	4
7	1	4	8	5	5	6	9	9	2
3	4	9	10	8	10	2	6	1	5
1	2	5	6	5	8	7	5	4	10
2	4	8	3	7	3	3	10	3	6
9	7	3	4	2	6	2	5	8	10
10	9	7	9	3	9	4	8	5	10
5	8	3	1	2	7	10	4	10	2
10	3	10	7	9	2	1	8	6	1

Puzzle 10

6	1	6	7	9	7	4	7	5	7
9	9	1	2	3	8	6	5	9	10
3	2	10	4	10	9	9	10	6	7
9	7	8	2	10	3	1	3	4	6
7	6	5	10	5	1	9	2	10	8
10	4	7	2	8	6	3	6	1	9
6	8	6	3	10	5	9	4	10	8
10	4	2	9	6	10	5	3	7	1
8	9	6	5	2	4	2	1	2	3
4	5	4	6	7	10	7	3	8	3

Puzzle 11

11	14	8	2	12	5	13	7	13	15	13	15	9	10	4	16	1
13	9	7	17	10	8	2	5	12	5	11	4	15	1	6	1	16
6	13	6	17	5	14	15	9	11	12	16	3	7	8	11	10	1
1	9	16	10	16	17	14	17	4	16	4	12	8	17	7	17	2
11	3	14	17	2	11	15	6	10	11	8	11	4	16	1	12	9
8	15	2	4	6	1	12	10	9	7	4	14	5	14	13	9	2
9	2	5	15	3	15	1	15	6	15	2	14	17	12	4	7	10
14	17	9	5	6	2	12	12	9	13	4	8	11	8	3	4	7
10	2	12	14	13	3	14	1	7	6	7	5	17	11	9	2	9
2	7	10	16	17	8	11	8	3	10	15	10	2	13	8	4	5
12	2	15	6	11	10	4	16	14	8	7	1	17	3	4	11	13
15	8	5	11	15	12	9	4	1	4	10	4	6	17	12	5	12
14	1	16	1	8	6	4	4	14	4	7	9	12	15	12	11	3
17	11	5	3	15	6	10	13	1	2	14	7	12	4	8	6	8
16	12	13	17	9	4	6	4	5	17	1	6	14	7	10	3	3
11	5	11	7	14	13	10	12	16	3	9	3	16	2	1	17	6
4	12	17	8	7	8	16	6	15	9	1	2	13	5	5	14	3

5	8	10	17	2	14	15	11	15	9	3	6	7	1	13	1	12
9	5	9	15	9	13	6	13	1	13	4	10	12	13	11	10	16
15	6	6	3	11	2	4	12	8	10	16	17	16	5	7	7	1
13	2	4	9	4	8	3	7	5	16	4	10	1	13	3	17	2
13	4	2	17	6	3	11	1	4	16	5	16	8	14	8	7	10
17	10	1	7	1	11	16	5	13	3	3	15	2	3	16	4	13
4	15	11	17	10	17	5	1	12	6	14	15	8	15	8	3	7
8	7	5	6	9	4	2	17	2	11	5	14	2	3	12	15	13
2	3	14	16	15	9	17	1	10	1	6	8	11	7	1	5	4
8	17	5	2	7	2	3	16	8	15	8	12	2	6	2	2	13
12	14	17	13	15	16	7	10	5	1	2	3	4	7	14	8	14
8	1	6	16	13	12	15	12	2	3	9	13	17	16	3	2	11
1	5	13	17	9	17	7	8	16	14	16	4	15	12	9	6	9
10	11	12	8	13	5	14	8	6	3	1	9	9	16	4	2	15
16	16	3	16	12	15	10	4	14	2	7	11	7	9	6	13	17
10	13	12	1	16	6	3	3	11	4	17	9	14	16	15	11	2
3	4	15	16	14	1	8	1	9	1	13	2	6	2	5	2	17

"A single arrow may break with ease,

but a bundle will surely succeed."

If at first you don't succeed, try, try again.

Concentration

専心

SLITHERLINK

Slitherlink is a beautifully pure Japanese puzzle, where the only rule is that you must draw a loop that passes by each clue the given number of times.

In more detail, the aim is to join some (but not necessarily all) of the dots with horizontal and vertical lines. Only a single loop can be created, and the loop cannot cross over or touch itself at any point. Each numbered clue must have that exact number of neighboring loop segments drawn around it. So, for example, a "3" clue would have lines that formed part of the loop drawn around three sides of it.

Mental Benefits

Despite its elegant simplicity, one of the most complex of all Japanese puzzles emerges from implications of these rules. You'll need to concentrate to solve the puzzles in this section, thinking carefully through the multiple ways you could solve each of the given numbers. You'll also need to pay close attention, checking carefully through each clue until you find somewhere to make progress. Being able to pay this type of diligent attention is very useful when you have a task that needs to get solved quickly.

GETTING STARTED

1.
```
3  3  3  3  2  3
2           3
3     0     2
2        0  1
1           1
2  1  2  3  2  2
```

- "0" clues can't have any neighboring loop segments, so make small "x"s to remember this.

- "3" clues only ever have four possibilities. You can try all four to discover that there is only one way to solve the top-left "3" that doesn't involve either immediately closing the loop or ending up with a line that can't connect.

2.

```
3 3 3 3 2 3
2         3
3  x0x    2
2    x0x  1
1         1
2 1 2 3 2 2
```

- The 3 at the top-left is fulfilled, so we can use a small "x" to remind ourselves of this. It's not really necessary here, but it can help to make a note of even "obvious" deductions when trying to finish your first puzzles.
- Because the loop can't travel through the "x" we just added, it must exit down from the left-hand side of the 3.
- This loop part is now at the top-left corner of another 3, which means that it must travel around the 3 either clockwise or anti-clockwise. Either way, the bottom- and right-hand sides of that 3 must be visited by the loop.

3.

```
3 3 3 3 2 3
2         3
3  x0x    2
2    x0x  1
1         1
2 1 2 3 2 2
```

- The 2 in the second square down in the leftmost column can now be solved. There are only two possibilities for the second line around it, but it cannot go on its right-hand side because, if it did, it would close the loop by forcing a solution to the 3 immediately beneath it. So the loop must travel across the bottom of the 2, and therefore downward from the left of the 3 beneath it.
- This means that the fourth square down in the first column is now solved—we can mark in "x"s in the remaining spots to remind ourselves of this.

4.

```
3 3 3 3 2 3
x2        3
3  x0x    2
2x   x0x  1
x
1         1
2 1 2 3 2 2
```

- Now you can extend the loop down past the 1 near the bottom of the leftmost column.
- This in turn lets you solve the 2 at the bottom-left.
- Continue looking for similar deductions, and trying out options to see if they succeed, until the loop is complete.

5.

```
3 3 3 3 2 3
2         3
3  0      2
2    0    1
1         1
2 1 2 3 2 2
```

- Once the loop is complete, the puzzle is solved.

Concentration: **SLITHERLINK**

29

Puzzle 1

```
3 2 3 3 3 3
3     0   1
2           2
1           3
1   0       2
3 3 2 2 3 3
```

Puzzle 2

```
3   3   3
2 3   1     3
2   1 1 2
  3 3 2     0
0   1     3 1
  0   1     0
```

Puzzle 3

Puzzle 4

```
2 2 2 2   0
3 3       1
1   3     1
  2   1     0
  3     2 2
0   1 2 2 3
```

```
2 1 1 2
2 1     0 2
    1     1 3
3 1     1
  2 0     2 2
    2 2 3 3
```

Puzzle 5

```
  3     3     3  2     2
1           0           3  2
  2     2     2     2     3
  2     3     2  1     2  3
  1              3     0
  2     2                 2
1  1     1  1        3     1
0     3     3     3     3
0  1              3              3
  0     2  2     2     3
```

Puzzle 6

```
  3                             3
  1     2  2        3     3
2     3     3  3        0     3
3  1     1     1        2  2
              0     2     2
  3     3     3
  2  2     1     1     2  2
2     2     3  3     3     3
  3     2     2  1     3
3                          2
```

Puzzle 7

```
.   .   .   .   .   .   .   .   .   .
      2         1       2
.   .   .   .   .   .   .   .   .   .
  2       2       3       3       1   2
. . .   .   .   .   .   .   .   .   .
  3  2  0       2       2
.   .   .   .   .   .   .   .   .   .
  2       2       1   2       1
.   .   .   .   .   .   .   .   .   .
  3       0                   3       2
.   .   .   .   .   .   .   .   .   .
  3       0                   2       3
.   .   .   .   .   .   .   .   .   .
      2       3   2       2       3
.   .   .   .   .   .   .   .   .   .
          2       1       1   2   1
.   .   .   .   .   .   .   .   .   .
  2  2       2       3       2       2
.   .   .   .   .   .   .   .   .   .
      3       3           2
.   .   .   .   .   .   .   .   .   .
```

Puzzle 8

```
.   .   .   .   .   .   .   .   .   .
      2       2       1
.   .   .   .   .   .   .   .   .   .
  3  1  1       3  0       3  1  1
.   .   .   .   .   .   .   .   .   .
      0       0  3       0       1
.   .   .   .   .   .   .   .   .   .
  2       1       2  1
.   .   .   .   .   .   .   .   .   .
  3           1                       0
.   .   .   .   .   .   .   .   .   .
  3                       3           1
.   .   .   .   .   .   .   .   .   .
              0  0       2       3
.   .   .   .   .   .   .   .   .   .
      1       0       1  1       2
.   .   .   .   .   .   .   .   .   .
  1  0  1       1  3       2  0  2
.   .   .   .   .   .   .   .   .   .
              2       3       2
.   .   .   .   .   .   .   .   .   .
```

```
.   .   .   .   .   .   .   .   .
   1   2   .   1   .   2   .   3   .
.   .   .   .   .   .   .   .   .   .
 2   .   3   .   .   3   .   1   3
.   .   .   .   .   .   .   .   .   .
 0   .   1   .   3   .   .   2   .
.   .   .   .   .   .   .   .   .   .
       3   2   .   1   .   2   .   3
.   .   .   .   .   .   .   .   .   .
 1   .   .   .   3   .   .   .   2
.   .   .   .   .   .   .   .   .   .
 1   .   .   0   .   .   .   .   3
.   .   .   .   .   .   .   .   .   .
 3   .   3   .   0   .   3   1   .
.   .   .   .   .   .   .   .   .   .
   2   .   .   0   .   0   .   2
.   .   .   .   .   .   .   .   .   .
 2   3   .   0   .   .   1   .   1
.   .   .   .   .   .   .   .   .   .
   1   .   2   .   1   .   3   2   .
.   .   .   .   .   .   .   .   .
```

```
.   .   .   .   .   .   .   .   .   .
   2   .   2   .   1   .   2   .   3
.   .   .   .   .   .   .   .   .   .
      1   2   2   .   2   .   2   .
.   .   .   .   .   .   .   .   .   .
 2   2   .   3   .   2   3   .   2   3
.   .   .   .   .   .   .   .   .   .
 3   .   3   2   .   .   .   .   3   2
.   .   .   .   .   .   .   .   .   .
 3   .   2   0   2   .   .   2   2
.   .   .   .   .   .   .   .   .   .
   1   3   .   .   2   2   1   .   2
.   .   .   .   .   .   .   .   .   .
 3   3   .   .   .   2   2   .   .   2
.   .   .   .   .   .   .   .   .   .
 2   1   .   2   2   .   2   .   2   3
.   .   .   .   .   .   .   .   .   .
   2   .   2   .   2   1   2   .   .
.   .   .   .   .   .   .   .   .   .
 3   .   2   .   2   .   2   .   1
.   .   .   .   .   .   .   .   .   .
```

```
3 3 2 2 2 . . . . .
. . . . 2 2 2 1 3 2
3 1 2 . 3 . . . . .
. . . . 3 2 3 2 3 .
. 2 1 3 . . . . . .
. . . . 0 . 0 0 . .
2 3 1 3 3 . . . . .
. . . . 1 2 3 1 3 .
. 3 1 . 2 . . . . .
. . . . . 1 3 1 . .
3 1 1 1 3 . . . . .
. . . . 0 . 2 3 1 .
1 0 1 0 0 1 . . . .
. . . . 3 2 3 2 3 .
```

```
3     1     2     3  2  1
   3     3     2           2
1     2  1  2     3     1
                     0     3
2  3  2  3  0
3                 1  3  3
   2  3  2     2           2
3           3     1  3  2
   2  3  2                 2
            3  0  2  2  3
2     1
   3     3     2  1  2     3
1           1     3     2
   3  2  3     1     3     3
```

HANJIE

Hanjie, also known by various other names, including griddler and nonogram, is a fun logic puzzle that involves shading squares to slowly reveal a hidden picture.

The numbers outside the grid reveal the number of shaded squares in the respective row or column, appearing in the order given. So, reading either from left to right or from top to bottom, they reveal the counts of each continuous sequence of shaded squares. All shaded squares are indicated by clues, and squares can only be shaded if they agree with the given clues.

If there is more than one sequence of shaded squares in a row or column, they must be separated by at least one empty square.

Mental Benefits

Hanjie might involve creating small works of pixel art, but getting there requires genuine concentration. You need to think about the various possible ways that a row or column could be solved, given its clue, and then work carefully back and forth between row and column clues, making small, iterative steps.

This type of concentration is a great skill to practice. Sometimes in life it's important to pay attention to the small details, and in hanjie you'll need to do this on a pixel-by-pixel basis!

1.

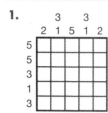

- The "5" clues on the top two rows must fill the full width of the 5-wide puzzle, so can be shaded in immediately.
- The same applies to the vertical "5" clue at the top of the grid.

2.

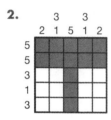

- Now you can see that the "2" clues in the leftmost and rightmost columns are already solved, so the rest of these columns must be empty. Make small "x"s to keep track of this.

3.

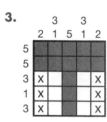

- The remainder of the puzzle is now easily solved, but consider first the "3 1" clues at the top of the puzzle. These must be solved by three shaded squares, followed by at least one empty square (which in this case has to be a single empty square as there isn't space for more than this), and then one shaded square.

4.

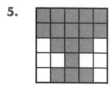

- There are only two squares left to solve, but checking the clues reveals that all of the given clues are now fulfilled—so these must be empty.

5.

- The completed puzzle.

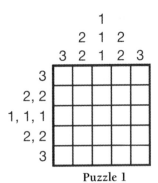

Puzzle 1

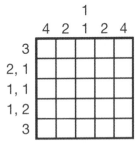

Puzzle 2

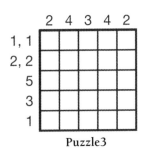

Puzzle3

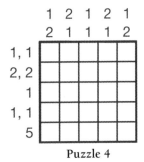

Puzzle 4

BRAIN TRAINING the JAPANESE WAY

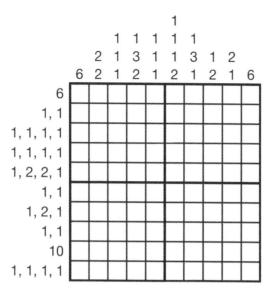

Puzzle 5

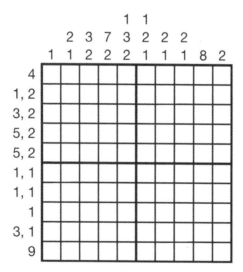

Puzzle 6

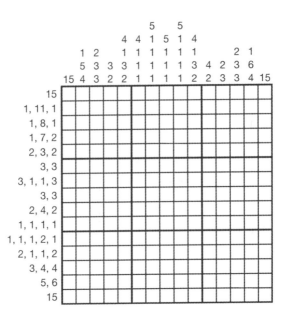

Puzzle 7

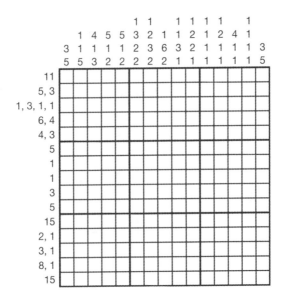

Puzzle 8

BRAIN TRAINING the JAPANESE WAY

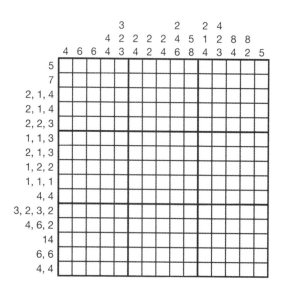

Puzzle 9

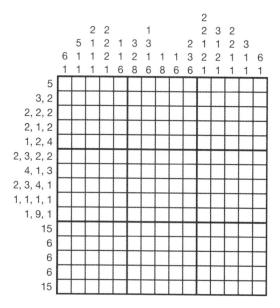

Puzzle 10

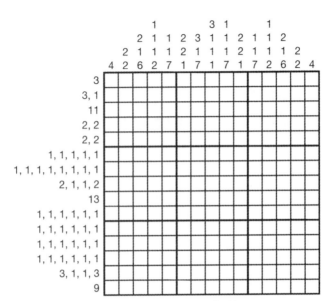

Puzzle 11

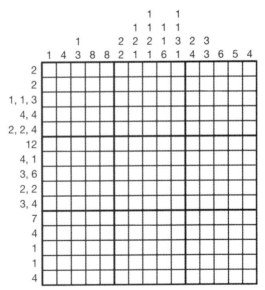

Puzzle 12

BRAIN TRAINING the JAPANESE WAY

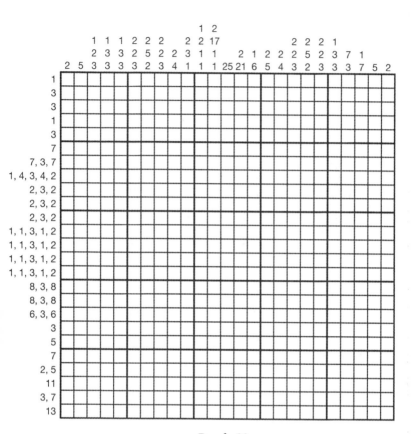

Puzzle 13

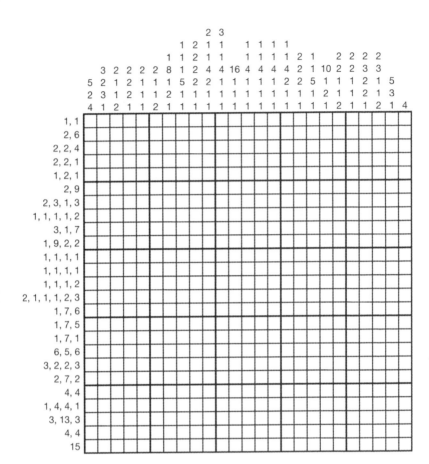

Puzzle 14

BRAIN TRAINING the JAPANESE WAY

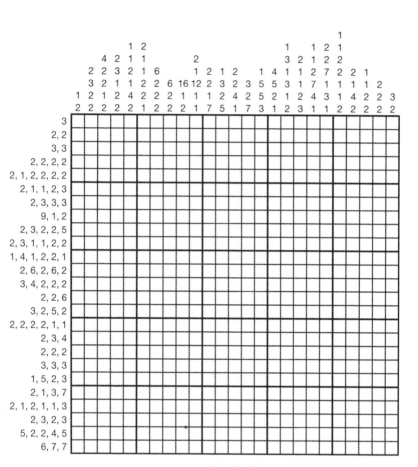

Puzzle 15

"You learn ten things just by learning one."

It might be hard at first, but you'll improve much faster than you expect.

Numerical Skills

数値スキル

CALCUDOKU

You might have come across calcudoku before under the brand name KenKen™, but it's all the same puzzle. To solve it, you place a number from 1 to 4 (or whatever the size the grid is) into the grid so that no number repeats in any row or column. Also, bold-lined regions in the puzzle provide various math results that must be fulfilled.

Specifically, each region has a numerical result printed at its top-left, along with the calculation that gives that result. These calculations can be addition, subtraction, multiplication or division. If a region is a "+" or "×" region, the numbers in that region must all add or all multiply together, respectively, to result in the given value. If it is a "-" or "÷" region, if you start with the largest number in that region and subtract or divide by the rest, respectively, then it must result in the given value.

- » In puzzles 9, 10, and 12 in this book, the operator (+, -, ×, ÷) is not given. This means that the result for each region could be from applying any of the four operators.

- » In puzzle 10, no clue at all is given for some regions—just to make it even trickier!

Mental Benefits

Numbers are all around us, but so often we hide behind a computer-calculated total—on a cash till, on a restaurant bill, or on our phones. And yet we all have basic math skills, which we can develop with just a little practice. Calcudoku is a great puzzle for practicing these skills, since it requires simple day-to-day mental arithmetic that helps get you used to doing calculations in your head. With time, if you solve enough calcudoku, these results start to become almost automatic.

1.

3÷		9+	
1-			
6×	7+		
		12×	

- This is a 4 × 4 puzzle, so we are placing 1 to 4 once each in every row and column.
- The "3÷" region must be solved by 3 and 1, in some order.
- The "12x" region must be solved by 3 and 4, in some order.
- The "7+" region must be solved by 1, 2, and 4, in some order.
- The "1-" region must be solved by 1, 2, and 4, in some order.
- We can make note of these options using small pencil numbers.

2.

3÷ 1 3	1 3	9+	
1- 1 2 4	1 2 4	1 2 4	
6×	7+ 1 2 4	1 2 4	1 2 4
		12× 3 4	3 4

- Numbers can't repeat in a row or column, so we can place 3s in the empty squares of the middle two rows.

3.

3÷ 1 3	1 3	9+	
1- 1 2 4	1 2 4	1 2 4	3
6× 3	7+ 1 2 4	1 2 4	1 2 4
		12× 3 4	3 4

- The placed 3s now let us solve the "3÷" and "12x" regions, since 3 is eliminated as an option from the top-left and bottom-right squares.

4.

3÷ 1	3	9+	
1- 2 4	1 2 4	1 2 4	3
6× 3	7+ 1 2 4	1 2 4	1 2
		12× 3	4

- The top-right square must now be 2, since there is already 1 and 3 in its row, and 4 in its column. You can then solve the last remaining square in the rightmost column.
- With 2 and 3 in the top-right region, you must now also have a 4 in it in order for it to sum to 9.
- Continue in a similar way until the puzzle is complete.

5.

3÷ 1	3	9+ 4	2
1- 4	2	1	3
6× 3	7+ 4	2	1
2	1	12× 3	4

- Now all the calculations are complete, and the puzzle is solved.

Puzzle 1

6+	11+		
	3+	6+	
11+			3+

Puzzle 2

12×	16×	4×	
		12×	
			12×
3×			

Puzzle 3

9+	2×		8+
8+		4×	
	8×		

Puzzle 4

144×	16×		
		9×	
1÷			

Puzzle 5

6+	24+	5+		11+	
		4+	7+		22+
			3+		
	6+		10+		
	6+				6+
7+		9+			

Puzzle 6

5×		12×	144×		
240×				15×	
	12×			60×	
		72×			
8×		90×	60×		
				2×	

Puzzle 7

144×	3×	2÷		160×	
			1−		
	40×			5×	12+
		5+			
16+			13+		
		7+			

Puzzle 8

80×		216×			60×
	3+		10×		
	33+			6×	
		4−		24+	
3+					

Puzzle 9

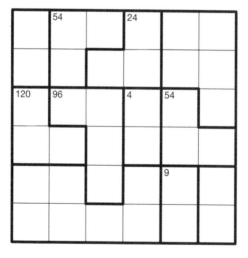

Puzzle 10

40×	14+	72×	336×			70×	
				7÷	180×		
1−	10×		17+				
		15+			12+	7÷	
7+			13+			32×	7+
336×	17+		5×		12+		
				18+		6×	48×

Puzzle 12

16			3		2		28
224		36	80	5	30		
						6	17
60		2		48			
	13			80		192	
		20	28				0
2							
	20		21		48		

KAKURO

Kakuro is a combination of a numerical crossword with the basic sudoku concept that numbers can't repeat.

Perhaps the easiest way to understand kakuro is to picture it as a normal, word-based crossword, with one clue for every word, but instead of writing one *letter* per square you now must write one *number* per square. Numbers must be in the range 1 to 9.

Clues are given in the shaded square immediately before the start of each "word" within the grid, and each clue is a number that gives the sum of the digits within its answer. Across clues are given above the diagonal lines; down clues are given below the lines.

Additionally, digits can't repeat within a single "word," so in a three-digit answer "1, 3, 4" would be okay but "3, 1, 3" would not.

Mental Benefits

When you first solve kakuro, it's all about working out what numbers can add up to the given totals, and then reasoning what must fit where as a result. With more practice, however, many of the maths-based parts start to become automatic. Even after solving just a few kakuro, you'll instantly know the solutions that have very limited combinations. For example, you'll know that $6 + 8 + 9 = 23$ without even a fraction of a second's thought (since in a 3-digit "word" with 23 as the clue, this is the only possible answer). Kakuro is therefore great practice for key mental arithmetic skills, since the more you start to add up numbers the sooner you will find yourself able to do it with less conscious thought.

GETTING STARTED

1.

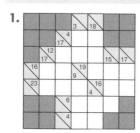

- The "3" and "4" clues can only be solved by 1 + 2 or 1 + 3, respectively. Mark in these options in pencil in the relevant squares.
- There is one square where the "3" and the "4" clues intersect (top-left). The only possibility in common is a 1, so this can be marked in as a final digit.

2.

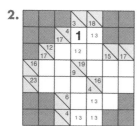

- The "3" and "4" clues with the placed 1 can now be fully solved.
- The "16" and "17" clues in the grid all cover only two squares, so must be solved by 7 + 9 or 8 + 9, respectively. Mark these options in in pencil.
- There are two squares where the "16" and "17" clues intersect, which must therefore contain 9s.

3.

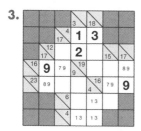

- You can now complete the rest of the numbers in the "16" and "17" clues.
- Continue solving in a similar way, working out what numbers can add up to each total, and cross-referencing the possible solutions to intersecting clues.

4.

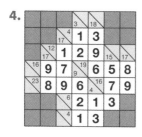

- Once all the "clues" are answered, the puzzle is solved.

Puzzle 1

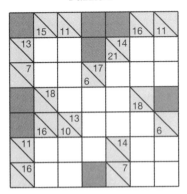

Puzzle 2

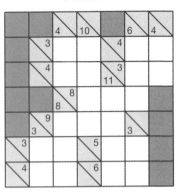

Puzzle 3

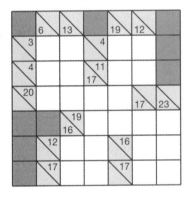

Puzzle 4

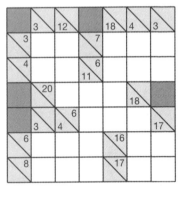

BRAIN TRAINING the JAPANESE WAY

Puzzle 5

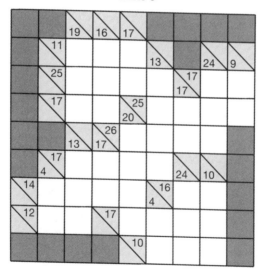

Puzzle 6

Puzzle 7

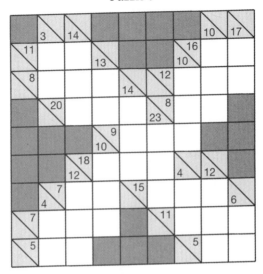

Puzzle 8

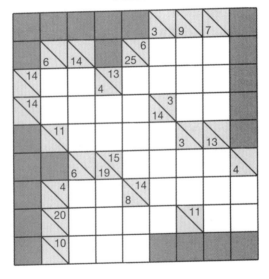

BRAIN TRAINING the JAPANESE WAY

Puzzle 9

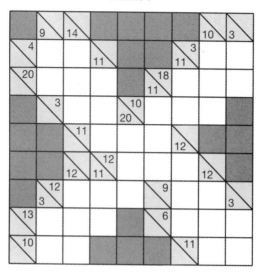

Puzzle 10

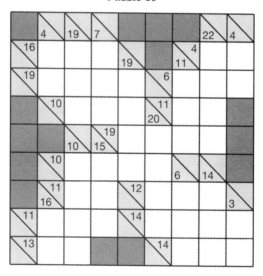

BRAIN TRAINING the JAPANESE WAY

Puzzle 12

FUTOSHIKI

The aim of futoshiki is to place a number from 1 to 5 (or whatever the size of the grid is) into each empty square, so that no number repeats in any row or column.

In futoshiki puzzles, all numbers must be placed so that they obey the inequality signs, which simply tell you that one number in a pair is larger than the other. It's easy to remember how these work: the arrows between squares always point at the smaller of the two numbers.

Mental Benefits

Futoshiki involves relative values of numbers, so, although it is not as mathematical as the other puzzle types in this chapter, it still requires you to consider the relationship between numbers more than you might otherwise in your daily life. Gaining extra familiarity with numbers is never a bad thing, even if it's just to help ensure you spot if a restaurant bill is incorrect, or so you can work out whether the supermarket discounts really are a good deal—or not.

GETTING STARTED

1.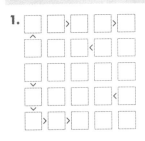

- There is a chain of five squares at the bottom-left that are all connected by inequality arrows, and what's more these all point in the same direction (allowing for them turning a corner), so you can write 1 to 5 into these squares.
- The 1 and 2 in the first column are then forced by the arrow.

2.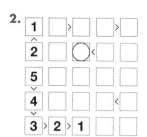

- In the bottom row there are only 4 and 5 left to place, so we can make a note of this in pencil, to remind us.
- The circled square can't contain 1 or 2 since these are already in either the row or column. It must be a number that's smaller than the number to its right. Therefore, it must be 3 or 4. The number to its right must be 4 or 5. We can make pencil-mark notes of these deductions too.

3.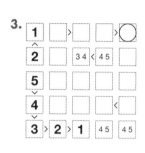

- The circled square can't contain 1 since there's already one in its row, and it must be a lower number than to its left, so it must contain 2, 3, or 4. The square to its left must be 3, 4, or 5.
- Notice how there are two squares in the fourth column that can only contain the same two numbers, 4 and 5. Although we don't know which way around they go, both 4 and 5 can be eliminated from the square at the top of the column. We can now pencil in 1 and 2 in the remaining squares in the fourth column, and place a 3 in the top square—which in turn forces a 2 in the circled square.

4.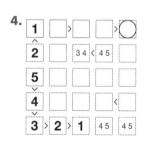

- The top row is now easy to complete, since the circled square must contain 4 or 5—but the inequality to its left forces it to be a 4. This then lets you place a 3 beneath it, and the third column can be completed.
- Now look at the inequality squares on the fourth row. The higher number can only be 3, since there is already a 4 and 5 in that row, and 2 in the column. From here the rest of the puzzle can be easily solved.

5.

- The completed puzzle.

Puzzle 1

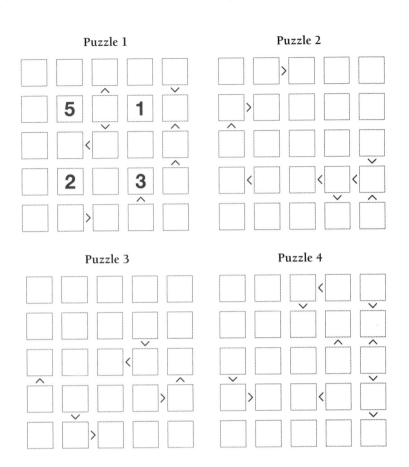

Puzzle 2

Puzzle 3

Puzzle 4

BRAIN TRAINING the JAPANESE WAY

Puzzle 5

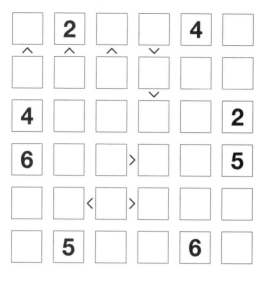

Puzzle 6

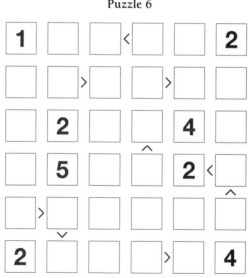

Puzzle 7

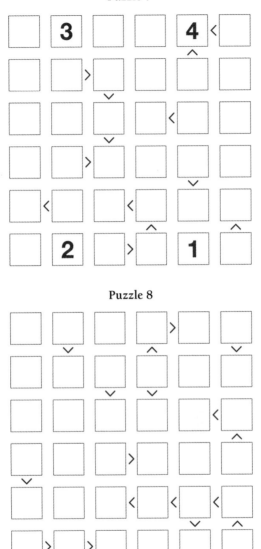

Puzzle 8

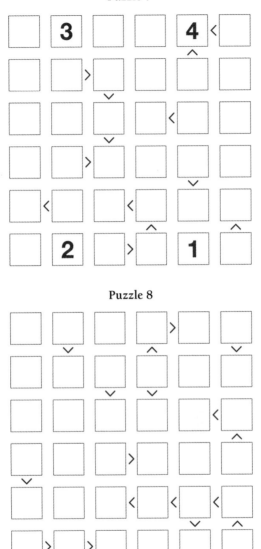

BRAIN TRAINING the JAPANESE WAY

Puzzle 9

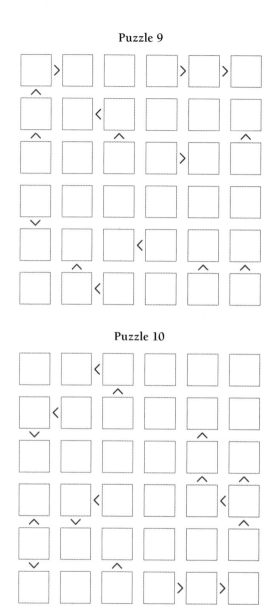

Puzzle 10

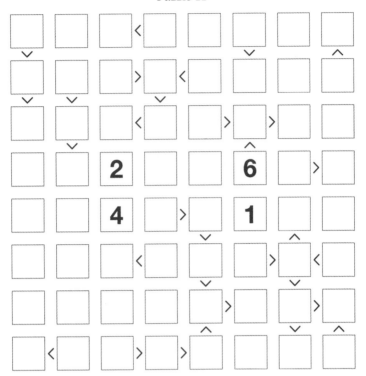

Puzzle 12

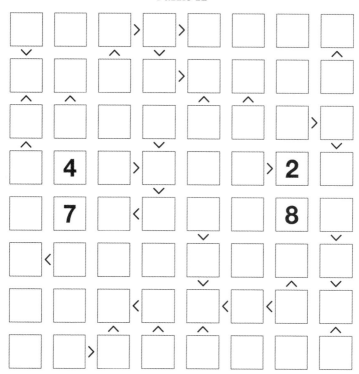

"With concentration, even the rocks will break before you."

It might be tricky at first, but with effort you will make it through.

Reasoning

推論

SHIKAKU

Shikaku is a popular Japanese puzzle that involves drawing along grid lines to divide the puzzle up into different areas. More specifically, you draw along some of the dashed grid lines to divide the grid into a set of rectangular and square regions.

Each region must have exactly one number in it, and that number must be equal to the exact number of squares contained within that region. Regions cannot overlap.

Mental Benefits

Like many things in life, shikaku puzzles are a lot easier to tackle if you start by taking a good look at what's in front of you. Some sensible, early decisions will make the puzzle much easier than if you just dive in and hope for the best. In most cases you can start with some logical deductions, which hugely simplify the remainder of the task. This type of reasoned, thoughtful approach to problem-solving will stand you in good stead for life.

1.

- The 1 regions must contain exactly one grid square with one number in, so their borders can be drawn in immediately.

2.

- The 6 clue has only one possible solution —a vertical rectangle. Draw this in.
- Now the 5 clue has only one possible solution—a horizontal rectangle.

3.

- The first square on the second row can only connect downward, so the 3 must run vertically down from this square.
- The 4 must be a 2 × 2 region. If it was a 4 × 1 then it would not be possible to place a region beneath it that contained a number.
- The 12 must be a 3 × 4 region—and the puzzle is now solved.

4.

- The completed puzzle.

Puzzle 1

4		4		4	
3				3	
2		2		2	
	3		3		
2				4	

Puzzle 2

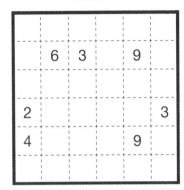

Puzzle 3

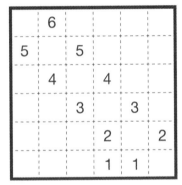

Puzzle 4

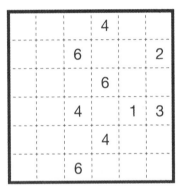

BRAIN TRAINING the JAPANESE WAY

Puzzle 5

	4							
							16	
		10						
				3		6		
2			3				14	
				4		6		
4	4				2			
		8			3			
		4	2	5				

Puzzle 6

			4		2	3		
4		3				3		
		6		3			3	
8	8				9			
3			8					5
	10							
						6		
4			2			3	3	

Puzzle 7

4					5			2
					5			
	16							
					18			
							3	
	4							
				6	6		3	
15					2			5
		3			3			

Puzzle 8

		5					3	
10					10			
	4							
					8		8	
	6	4					5	
							10	
2	2							
	9							4
	2		2	6				

Puzzle 9

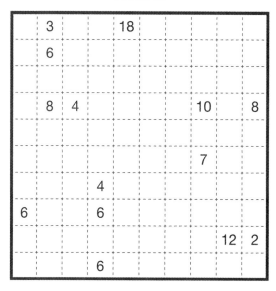

Puzzle 10

							6						6		
							6								
			6				6						6	6	
				5								6			
				5					5						
6									5			6	6		
6	6											6	6		
						6	6			5					
	6														6
				6											6
		5													
		5							6		6	6	6		
	6	6													
		6						6	6						5
														5	

1			3	8										7
	2		2					6						
2		3												
10			4											
				5										
					6									
		4				7								
			5					8						
	7							9						
					4				10					
			8							11				7
		9									12			
	10											13		
13													14	
														15

PURENRUPU

There's a reason that the name of this puzzle translates to "pure loop," since the aim is just that simple: draw a single loop across the grid that visits every white square. And that's it!

Specifically, draw a single loop made up of horizontal and vertical lines that travel between the centers of squares. The loop can only enter each square once, so it cannot cross or touch itself, and it also cannot double back on itself once it enters a square. The loop must enter *every* white square exactly once, and cannot enter the shaded squares.

Mental Benefits

Purenrupu, like many tasks in life, benefits from being broken down into smaller tasks. It would be a tough puzzle to solve if, once you started drawing, you had to complete the loop without lifting your pen. Instead, consider different parts of the puzzle as miniature, smaller tasks, and identify first the various bits of the loop that must be forced. Then, when you take a step back and consider the wider puzzle, you will have already solved various smaller parts and the overall task becomes a lot simpler. It's great practice for tackling a range of tasks in life.

1.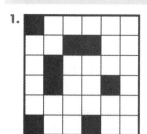

- In the area around the top-left, a "corridor" is formed that is only one square wide—so, since every square must be visited, the loop must pass through here.
- There's a similar, but much shorter, "corridor" near the bottom-right. This can be drawn in too.

2.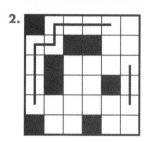

- On the bottom row, there are two white areas that are each two squares wide. Because the loop must both enter and exit these, you can draw the loop going in and coming out of each of these areas.
- In order for the loop to visit every square, you can then connect these new loop parts to the existing loop sections that were drawn in the previous step.
- In the center of the puzzle, the loop must travel in and out of the square against the corner formed by the shaded squares.

3.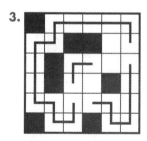

- Now you can solve the rest by visual inspection, and thinking about how the loop segments must join up to make a single loop.

4.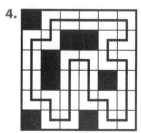

- Once the loop is complete, the puzzle is solved.

Reasoning: PURENRUPU

Puzzle 1

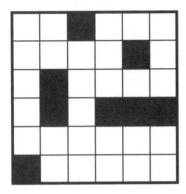

Puzzle 2

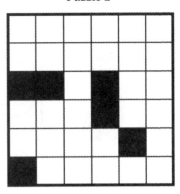

Puzzle 3

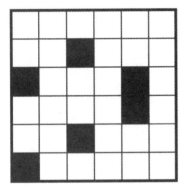

Puzzle 4

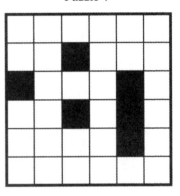

BRAIN TRAINING the JAPANESE WAY

Puzzle 5

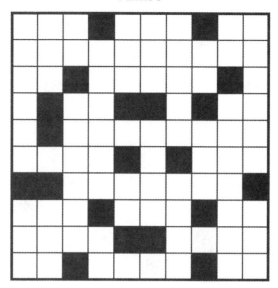

Puzzle 6

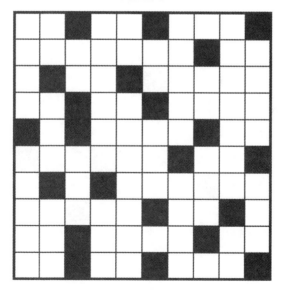

Puzzle 7

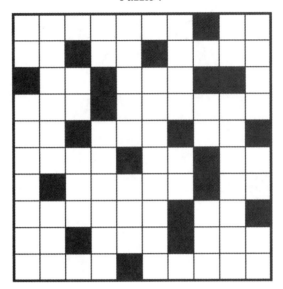

Puzzle 8

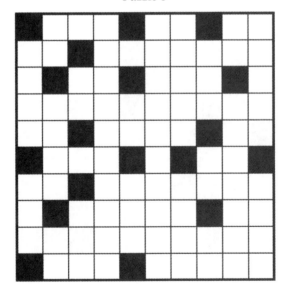

BRAIN TRAINING the JAPANESE WAY

Puzzle 9

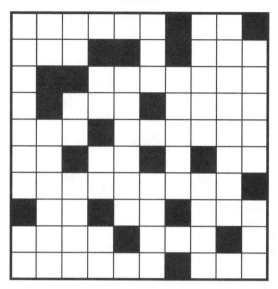

Puzzle 10

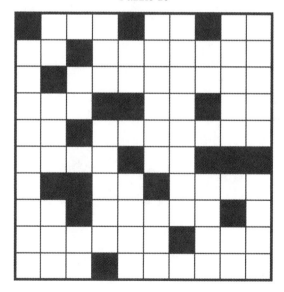

Puzzle 11

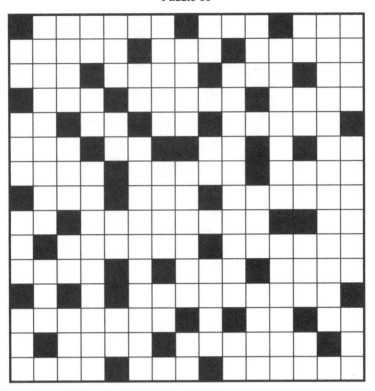

BRAIN TRAINING the JAPANESE WAY

Puzzle 12

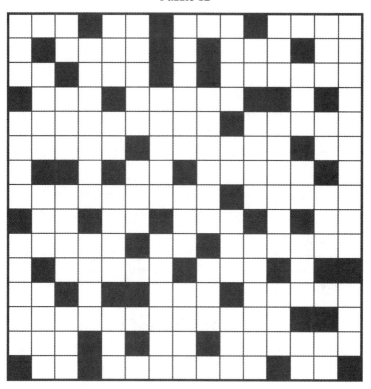

MASYU

The aim of masyu is to draw a single loop across the whole grid that passes through the center of every circle, using only horizontal and vertical lines.

The loop doesn't have to visit every square, but it must pass through all circled squares. There are two types of circle, and they each have different rules:

» The loop must pass *straight through* every square containing a *white circle, and* the loop *must* turn in either one or both of the immediately preceding and immediately following squares.

» The loop must make a *90-degree turn* in every square containing a *shaded* circle, and it *must* travel straight through both of the immediately preceding and immediately following squares without turning.

Mental Benefits

Masyu is a good test of your ability to keep a number of constraints in your head. Your focus will switch between the loop constraints and the need to obey the rules of white and shaded circles, and it can be easy to miss something. Masyu is good practice for taking it slowly and carefully, and thinking things through as you make progress.

GETTING STARTED

1.

- The white circles against the puzzle edge must have the loop travel through parallel to the edge.
- The shaded circle must have one part of the loop exit perpendicular to the edge, extending straight through the square below it. Where a shaded and white circle are neighbors on an edge, the shaded circle can be fully solved.

BRAIN TRAINING the JAPANESE WAY

2.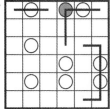

- Remembering that there is only one continuous loop, the top-right parts of the loop must connect.
- The two white circles in column 4 cannot have a vertical line through them, otherwise they would connect to the existing loop above and the upper circle would not have a turn in at least one neighboring square, as required.

3.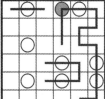

- There are now four loop ends that must extend into neighboring squares in order to remain connected. Draw these in.

4.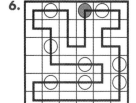

- Now consider the fact that if you were to draw a horizontal line through the middle circle in the second column, you would end up having to create a very small separate loop at the top left. Only one loop is allowed, so this must be wrong—and that circle must have a vertical line through it.
- Similarly, we can mark a small "×" between lines to show that we can't connect the two ends in the fourth and fifth rows together.

5.

- Now think about what would happen if we drew a vertical line through the last remaining unused circle. If you did this, you'd create two loops—one on the left, and one on the right. So this must be wrong.
- Armed with this information, you can now complete the rest of the puzzle.

6.

- The completed puzzle.

Puzzle 1

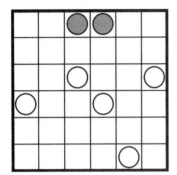

Puzzle 2

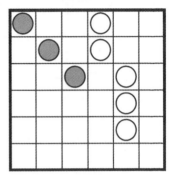

Puzzle 3

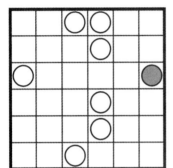

Puzzle 4

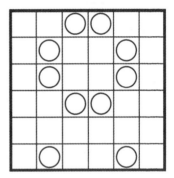

BRAIN TRAINING the JAPANESE WAY

Puzzle 5

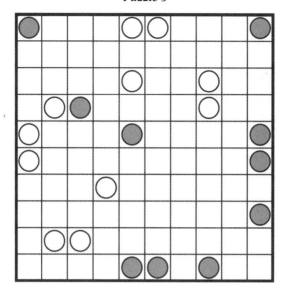

Puzzle 6

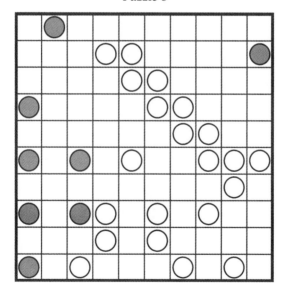

Puzzle 7

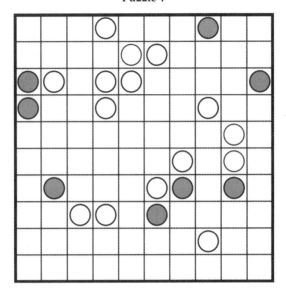

Puzzle 8

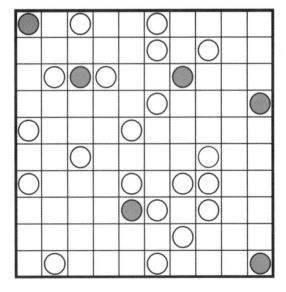

BRAIN TRAINING the JAPANESE WAY

Puzzle 9

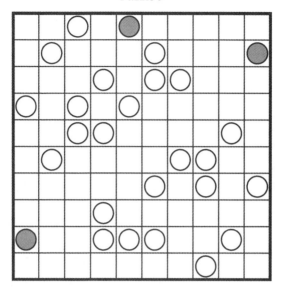

Puzzle 10

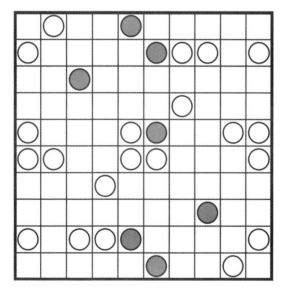

Puzzle 11

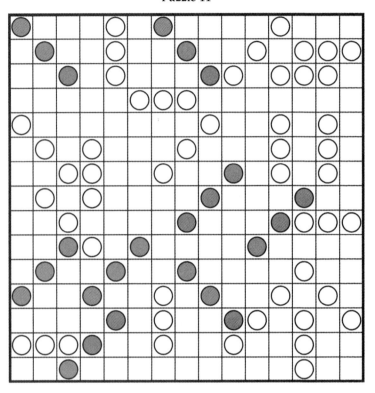

BRAIN TRAINING the JAPANESE WAY

Puzzle 12

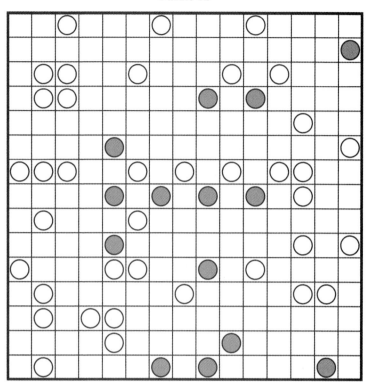

"A lighthouse does not

illuminate its own tower."

Make the obvious deductions first.

Observation

観察

NUMBERLINK

Numberlink is an elegant Japanese puzzle with a simple aim: draw paths to join each pair of identical numbers, ensuring that the paths don't cross.

The paths that join numbers must travel horizontally or vertically between the centers of squares, and they cannot cross over or touch each other at any point. No more than one path can enter each grid square, although conversely it is not a requirement that every grid square is used. (Despite this, however, in most published numberlink puzzles it actually *is* the case that all grid squares are used—but you can't assume this.)

Mental Benefits

Solving numberlink puzzles often requires you to take an overview of the entire puzzle grid and think about how you can simultaneously connect all of the number pairs. Trying to route all of the paths simultaneously in your head can lead to a frustrating sense of not quite being able to comprehend the puzzle fully, but it's good to practice this skill with something as relatively unimportant as a puzzle. Being able to tie together lots of separate threads, and form an overview of the whole of a task, is an important life skill.

1.

● Start with a couple of small forced deductions. The numbers at the top-right and bottom-left each have only one empty square they can connect to, so they must each have paths that extend out.

2.

● Now you need to try and conceive of an overall solution to the puzzle. For this small puzzle, you can probably see that if you join the 2s and 3s via the shortest possible paths, there will be enough space left to connect the 1s. Join the 2s and 3s.

3.

● Now there is only one possible route left for the 1, and the puzzle can be fully solved.

● If you get stuck on a puzzle, it is worth experimenting with connecting nearby numbers as directly as possible, and seeing what would result from this.

4.

● The completed puzzle.

Observation: NUMBERLINK

101

Puzzle 1

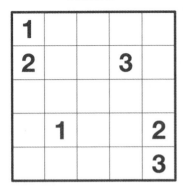

Puzzle 2

Puzzle 3

Puzzle 4

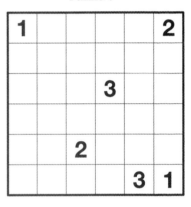

BRAIN TRAINING the JAPANESE WAY

							1	2
1		3						4
								5
			6		7	3	4	
		8					5	
		9	10			8	6	
2							10	
7			9					

1			2			3		4	5
6									
				7		5			4
					1		8	9	8
			2						
			3		7			9	
	6								

	1		2	3	2		4	5
				1				
6					7			
8				9				
6							5	
				10				4
	8			9				
					10		7	3

Puzzle 8

	1			2			2	
3						1		
	4			5	6			6
5	7						8	
4			9					
						3		
						8		
	7							
		10	9					10

Puzzle 9

		1		2	3			
	4						5	6
								7
		1						
						7		
						8		
		8		6		9		
	4	3			5			
	10				9			
			2	10				

Puzzle 10

1		2	3					
4			5			5		
			3					
		1						
6			4	7		7		
		8					8	
						9		
		6		10	2			
10			9					

Puzzle 11

	2											
		1										
			3						7			
	10				4							
		9										
					5							
			8									
					10							
					5				7			
								6	3	6		
	12	13		13	11		4			2		
					12						8	
						11					9	1

BRAIN TRAINING the JAPANESE WAY

	1			2	3	4							
	5						1						
	2						6		7				
							8		9				
					7								
					10			11	8				
				12	13			5					
								14					
				11		12							
				10		13						15	
						6						3	
							15	14	9			4	

HASHI

Hashi is sometimes known in English as "bridges," due to the fact that it can be envisioned as a puzzle that involves connecting circular islands with bridges. More prosaically, however, the aim is to draw horizontal and vertical lines to join all of the circled numbers into a single connected network. No more than two lines can connect any given pair of circles.

Each circled number needs to have the matching number of horizontal or vertical lines drawn from it—and every one of those lines must connect to another circled number. The lines cannot cross over one another, or over another circle, and all number clues must be exactly fulfilled in the finished puzzle.

Additionally, in the completed puzzle, if you were to place your finger on a circle then you must be able to reach any other circle simply by sliding your finger along connected lines.

Mental Benefits

In hashi, connecting circles can sometimes be some distance apart, so you need to ensure you don't miss any possible connections as you solve the puzzle by making good use of your observation skills. You also need to look out for circles that can only connect in a very limited way—often these are the place to get started on a puzzle. Similarly, in life, keeping a good overview of a task, while finding the specific areas that will most easily help you get started on a problem, is a valuable skill.

1.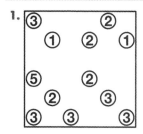

- The 5 on the left must have at least one line traveling up, to the right, and down—otherwise it would need more than 2 lines connecting in one direction.
- Similarly, the 3 at the bottom-right must have one line in each possible direction. However, as the line up connects to a 1, which can have no more lines connected, the third line must connect out to the left.

2.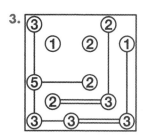

- The 3 in the middle of the bottom row must now also connect to the left.
- The 2 near the bottom-left must now have both its lines connecting to the right, since lines can't cross over one another.
- The 3 that the 2 just connected to must have its remaining line connecting upward.

3.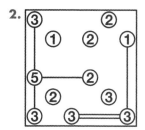

- The final line from the 3 at the bottom-left must go up, otherwise the 3 to its right would have four lines connected to it.
- The 1 near the top-left must connect to the 2 to its right, which must in turn connect down.
- The 3 at the top-left now has only one way to be completed, and the puzzle is solved.

4.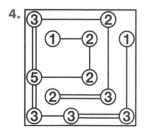

- The completed puzzle.

Puzzle 1

Puzzle 2

Puzzle 3

Puzzle 4

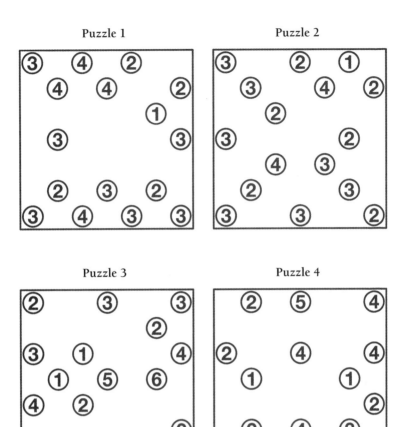

BRAIN TRAINING the JAPANESE WAY

Puzzle 5

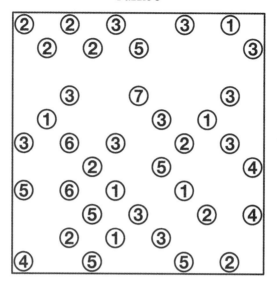

Puzzle 6

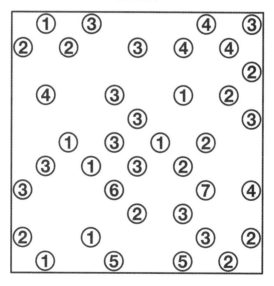

Puzzle 7

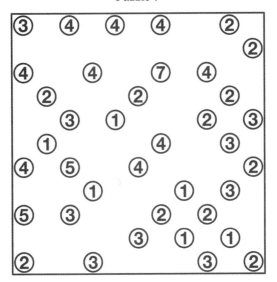

Puzzle 8

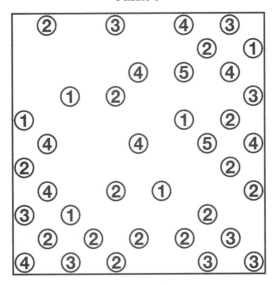

BRAIN TRAINING the JAPANESE WAY

Puzzle 9

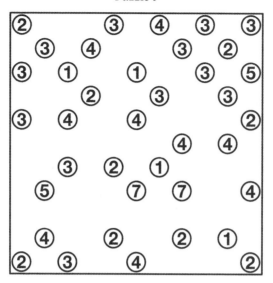

Puzzle 10

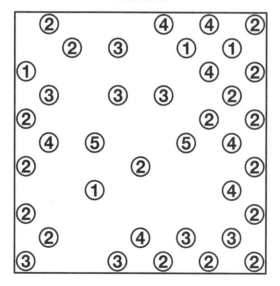

Puzzle 11

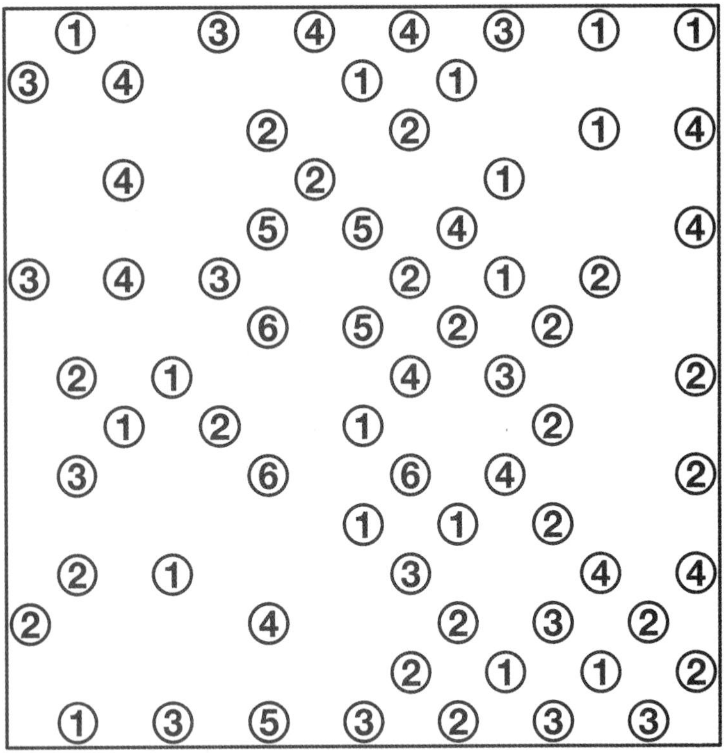

Puzzle 12

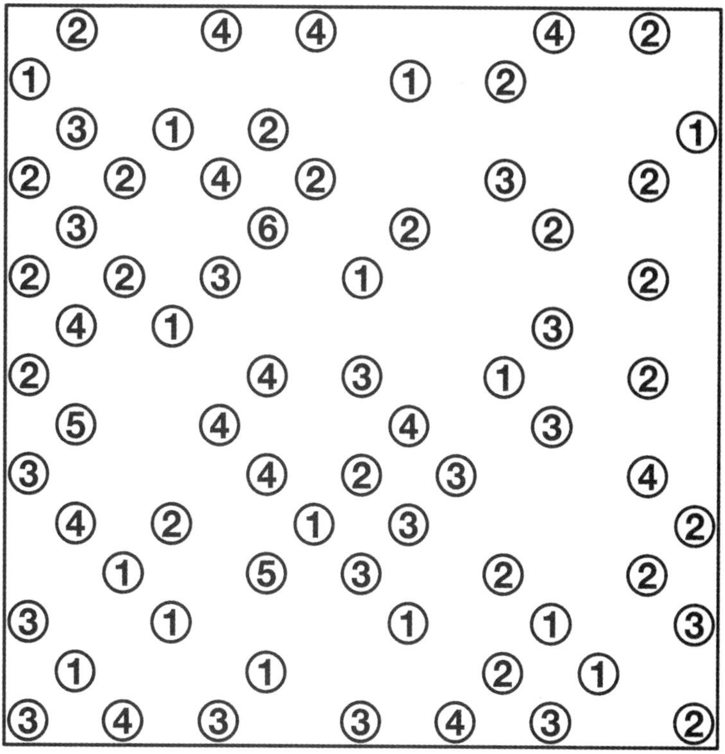
2 4 4 4 2
1 1 2
3 1 2 1
2 2 4 2 3 2
3 6 2 2
2 2 3 1 2
4 1 3
2 4 3 1 2
5 4 4 3
3 4 2 3 4
4 2 1 3 2
1 5 3 2 2
3 1 1 1 3
1 1 2 1
3 4 3 3 4 3 2

NURIKABE

Nurikabe is one of the best known of a class of Japanese puzzles involving shading squares within a grid. The overall aim, however, is to form regions of *unshaded* squares. Each region must contain a single number, indicating the exact number of unshaded squares in that region. All squares outside regions must be shaded.

The unshaded regions can be any shape but they must be bordered on all sides by either the edge of the grid or by a shaded square. Numbers can't be shaded, and nor can you add any extra numbers to the grid.

All of the shaded squares must form a single connected area. This means you could start on any shaded square and slide your finger to any other shaded square, all without moving diagonally or passing over any unshaded square.

Finally—but importantly—you cannot shade all four squares for any given 2 × 2 area of grid squares (or larger).

Mental Benefits

Nurikabe is a fantastic puzzle, since it requires you to consider a large number of possible observations, while sometimes also simultaneously considering how the overall puzzle could come together. However, despite this complexity, it can also typically be subdivided into a series of smaller tasks, simply by thinking about the implications of each of the various rules in turn. In this way it encourages you to learn to think flexibly when solving a complex problem.

1.

- The 1 clues must have either a shaded square or the edge of the puzzle on all four sides, so four squares can be shaded in.
- The 5 region at the bottom cannot extend to the left, as it would leave a square at the bottom-left that would have to be shaded (so the 2 and 5 regions did not touch) but which could not connect to the rest of the shaded squares in the puzzle. So you can shade in the square to the left of the 5.
- Similarly, the 2 region cannot extend into the square to its right, as it would create a two-square shaded area beneath it that could not connect to the other shaded squares.

2.

- Since all shaded squares must connect, the two shaded areas in the top-left corner can be extended into their neighboring empty squares.
- All 2 × 2 areas must contain at least one unshaded square, which means that the 5 region must visit all of the 2 × 2 areas labeled with circles—it must enter the squares indicated by the bold line. We don't yet know whether it goes up or right from the 5 clue itself, however. It cannot reach any further up, though, so the remaining squares in the puzzle must be shaded.

3.

- To finish the 5 region, one of the two question-marked squares must be shaded. To avoid a 2 × 2 shaded area, it must be the upper of the two options.

4.

- The completed puzzle.

Observation: NURIKABE

117

Puzzle 1

5				
4				
3				1

Puzzle 2

		12		
			1	
		1		

Puzzle 3

3				9
				5

Puzzle 4

3				2
		2		
7				

Puzzle 5

		1			1			4	
	2			3			3		
		5						1	
	3						3		
		2			3			4	
	4			1			1		

Puzzle 6

					2				
				4					
					2				
2					5			4	
	3			6					2
				2					
				4					
				5					

Puzzle 7

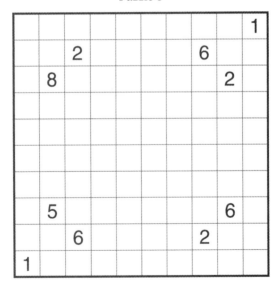

Puzzle 8

BRAIN TRAINING the JAPANESE WAY

Puzzle 9

9								6
	1			4		1		
		1						
			1					
				1				
					1			
	5		1			1		
6								12

Puzzle 10

				5				
			6					
								5
	5			5				
5			6					
				5				
			5					

									3			
								3				
									7			
								3				
									39			
								8				
									35			
								16				

Puzzle 12

					3			1			1	
				1			2				5	
	6											
3						3			2			
					5			5				
			3								4	
		3								3		
					1		1					1
			2		3							
6		1							3			
							2					2
		3			1	3						2
			4						6			2

"The productive plant is heavy,

and hangs its head."

Don't hide your talents.

Creative Thinking

創造的思考

YAJILIN

Yajilin is a fun, loop-drawing puzzle that involves shading squares and drawing a continuous loop across the grid.

Specifically, you must draw a single loop that enters *every* square that is neither shaded nor a given clue. It cannot exit a square through the same side it entered. The loop can only enter each square once, which means it cannot cross over or touch itself. It can also only travel horizontally or vertically between squares.

You can shade any completely empty square you like, as long as two shaded squares don't touch to the left, right, above or below.

Arrow clues are given in the grid, and these reveal the exact number of shaded squares—in the same row or column—that are in the direction pointed to by the arrow. It's important to note, though, that not all shaded squares are necessarily pointed to by arrows.

Mental Benefits

With its combination of shading squares *and* finding a loop, yajilin requires the creative mixing of two separate aims: fulfilling the given clues, while still being able to draw a valid loop. Finding the solution involves combining these two visual factors, so it is a great puzzle for exercising your creative problem-solving skills.

GETTING STARTED

1.

- The 1↑ at the top-left points at only one square, so shade that square.
- Shaded squares can't touch, and the loop must visit all empty squares, so the loop must go into—and out of—the square next to the shaded square.
- The loop can't do a u-turn in a single square, so the squares between the clues in the first column *cannot* be shaded. Mark this with "x"s.

BRAIN TRAINING the JAPANESE WAY

2.

- The loop must go in and out of the "x" squares and, since there can be only one loop in the grid, it must exit upward out of that area, joining to the existing loop segment.
- The loop can't do a u-turn in the bottom-left square, so it must be shaded and have a loop segment next to it.

3.

- The 2↑ clue on the right needs two shaded, non-touching squares above it. Remembering that a loop can't do a U-turn in and out of a square, these shaded squares can be placed, along with a further part of the loop through the top-right section of the grid.
- The bottom-right can be solved in the same way as the bottom-left.

4.

- The square marked with a "?" can't be shaded, since the loop just above it to the left would need to split and go both down and to the right simultaneously, which isn't possible. So the 1↓ clue can be solved, and more loop drawn in.

5.

- If either of the remaining white squares at the top was shaded, the loop wouldn't connect—so they must both be visited by the loop.

6.

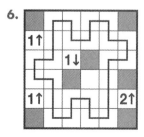

- The completed puzzle.

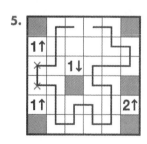

Creative Thinking: YAJILIN

Puzzle 1

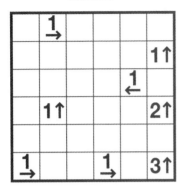

Puzzle 2

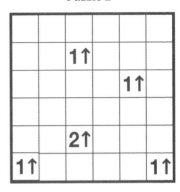

Puzzle 3

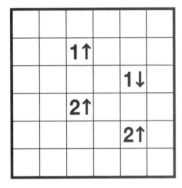

Puzzle 4

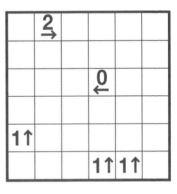

BRAIN TRAINING the JAPANESE WAY

Puzzle 5

				1↑				
	4↓						2⇐	
				2↑				
	3↓						1↑	
				3↑				
	2↓						2↑	
				4↑				
	1↓						3↑	

Puzzle 6

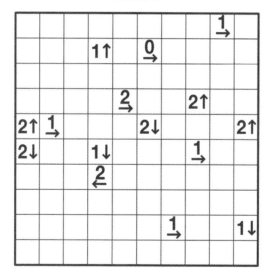

Puzzle 7

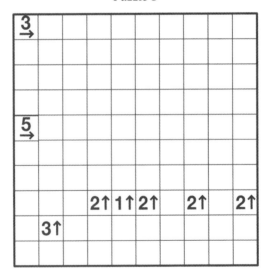

Puzzle 8

BRAIN TRAINING the JAPANESE WAY

Puzzle 9

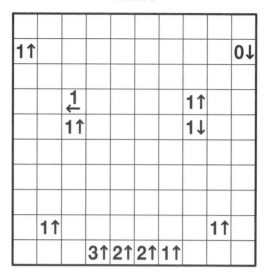

Puzzle 10

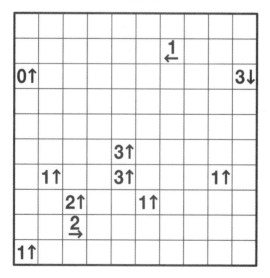

Puzzle 11

				2→			2→			2→				
								2→						
	2↑				2↑			2←				2↑		
					2↑	2→		2→		2↑				
								2↓						
		2↑	2↑	2↑	2↑			2↓		2↑	2↑	2↑		
										2↑		2←	2←	
						2←								
								2←						
							2↑		2→	2↑		2↑		
				2←										

Puzzle 12

AKARI

Akari is a relaxing Japanese puzzle, involving placing lamps to illuminate all of the empty squares within a puzzle. Lamps can be placed in any white square and always shine horizontally and vertically, illuminating all of the squares they can reach. Light cannot travel through the black squares.

Some of the black squares contain numbers. These tell you exactly how many lamps must be placed in the squares that touch them directly—above, below, to the left, or to the right.

Your aim is to place lamps until every white square is illuminated. But there's one extra rule that makes the puzzle trickier than it appears: lamps *cannot* shine on other lamps.

Mental Benefits

Some puzzles are so delightfully visual that you can look at their grids and almost immediately start to imagine how they might be solved, in a way that could never apply to a number-placement puzzle such as sudoku. Akari is one of these.

This kind of creative thinking helps highlight how creativity is not just about making art, but a process we can all use in many aspects of our day-to-day thinking. You have unlimited creative powers, and the puzzles in this chapter can help you release them.

1.

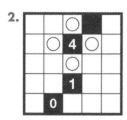

- The "4" clue is easily solved, since the placement of four lights around it is fixed.

2.

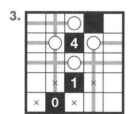

- Draw in the light shining from each lamp as you go. This helps you keep track of which white squares are still to be illuminated.
- Lamps can't be placed in illuminated squares, and nor can they go next to the "0." We can keep track of this by marking "x"s.

3.

- The three given clues are all solved. We still need to illuminate two squares in the leftmost column, so we need a lamp here. It can't go in the bottom-left square, so it is forced to go one square above that.
- Similarly, we need to illuminate the rest of the bottom row by placing a lamp at the bottom-right.

4.

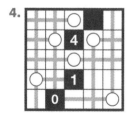

- Now all squares are lit, and the puzzle is solved.

Puzzle 1

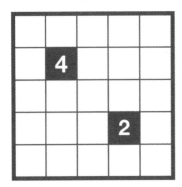

Puzzle 2

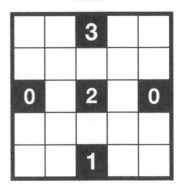

Puzzle 3

Puzzle 4

BRAIN TRAINING the JAPANESE WAY

Puzzle 5

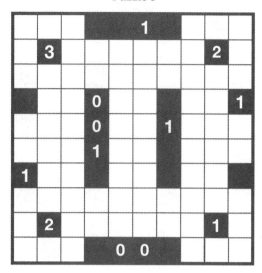

Puzzle 6

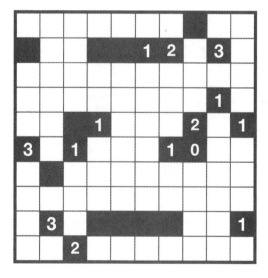

Puzzle 7

Puzzle 8

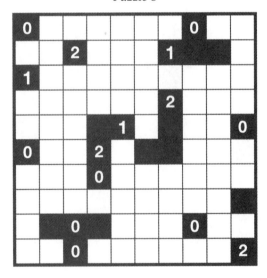

Puzzle 9

Puzzle 10

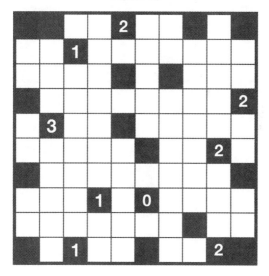

BRAIN TRAINING the JAPANESE WAY

Puzzle 12

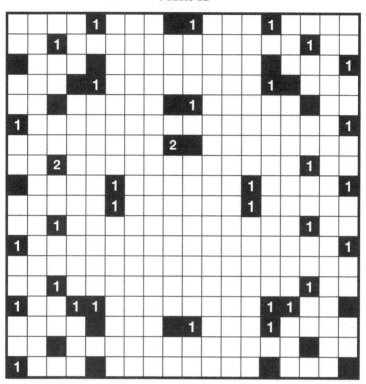

TENTAI SHOW

Tentai show is a dramatic line-drawing puzzle with an extra twist: once complete, it reveals a hidden picture.

Your aim is to divide the grid into regions by drawing along the dashed lines, so that every region has exactly one dot contained within it. What's more, each of the dots must be in the exact center of its region, *and* the region must be drawn so that it would be *identical* if it was rotated 180 degrees around that dot. Every grid square must be inside exactly one region.

Once complete, shade in the regions with gray dots to reveal a simple hidden picture.

Mental Benefits

You'll need smart visual thinking and some creative reasoning to crack these puzzles. The symmetrical shapes can be complex, and cover many more squares than in the tutorial puzzle, opposite. The secret, like in life, is not to be bounded by your assumptions—try out options that seem unlikely, since you never know when they might turn out to be the right choice!

GETTING STARTED

1.

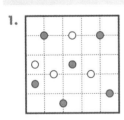

- Dots on the intersection of four grid squares must be in a region that includes at least all four of those squares, for example the two gray dots on the first horizontal dashed line.
- Dots on the intersection of two grid squares must be in a region that includes at least both of those squares, for example the white dot on the first horizontal dashed line.

BRAIN TRAINING the JAPANESE WAY

- If a region is bounded on one side, for example by the edge of the grid, then a symmetrical border can be drawn on the opposite side of the central dot. This applies, for example, to the two dots in the leftmost column.
- When a region cannot expand any further without encroaching on a neighboring region, there must be a border between them. This applies, for example, to the gray dot in the very center of the grid, which cannot expand to its left or right.
- Remember that regions must be identical if rotated 180 degrees, so we can, for example, mark the bottom-right corner of the region containing the white dot in the fourth column.

2.

- The rightmost square on the third row must belong to the white dot that is partially in the square to its left, since if it connected to the gray dot below then that region could not be symmetrical around its dot. This then lets the remaining regions be completed.

3.

- Now that the region boundaries have been found, shade those with gray dots to reveal a simple smiley face.

4.

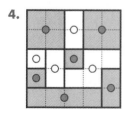

- The completed puzzle.

Puzzle 1

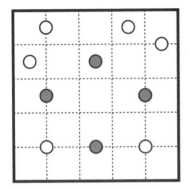

Puzzle 2

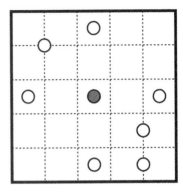

Puzzle 3

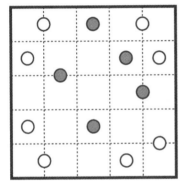

Puzzle 4

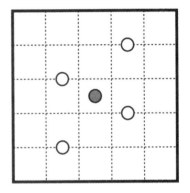

BRAIN TRAINING the JAPANESE WAY

Puzzle 5

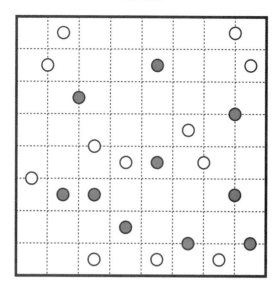

Puzzle 6

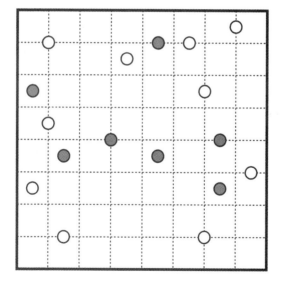

Puzzle 7

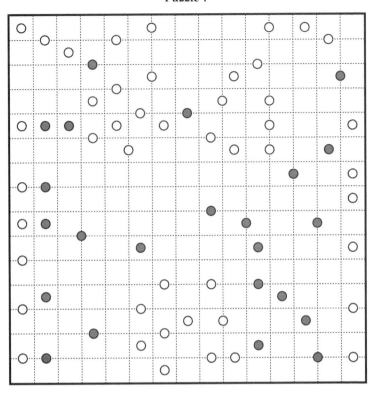

BRAIN TRAINING the JAPANESE WAY

Puzzle 8

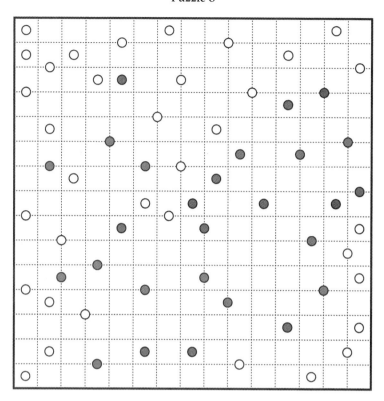

The Answers

答え

"Even monkeys fall from trees."

Everyone makes mistakes.

Sudoku, puzzle 1

2	4	6	5	3	1
1	5	3	4	2	6
5	3	1	6	4	2
4	6	2	1	5	3
3	1	5	2	6	4
6	2	4	3	1	5

Sudoku, puzzle 2

2	5	3	6	1	4
6	4	1	3	2	5
5	6	2	1	4	3
1	3	4	2	5	6
4	1	6	5	3	2
3	2	5	4	6	1

Sudoku, puzzle 3

4	3	1	5	2	6
2	5	6	1	3	4
6	2	5	4	1	3
1	4	3	6	5	2
3	1	4	2	6	5
5	6	2	3	4	1

Sudoku, puzzle 4

1	4	2	6	3	5
5	6	3	1	4	2
6	3	5	4	2	1
4	2	1	3	5	6
2	1	4	5	6	3
3	5	6	2	1	4

Sudoku, puzzle 5

6	7	2	1	4	3	5	9	8
8	4	3	9	5	7	1	2	6
9	5	1	8	6	2	7	3	4
7	1	4	3	9	5	6	8	2
2	9	5	6	7	8	4	1	3
3	6	8	2	1	4	9	5	7
5	2	9	4	8	6	3	7	1
1	8	6	7	3	9	2	4	5
4	3	7	5	2	1	8	6	9

Sudoku, puzzle 6

6	8	7	3	2	5	9	4	1
4	2	9	8	6	1	3	5	7
1	3	5	7	9	4	6	8	2
2	9	1	4	8	3	7	6	5
7	5	8	6	1	2	4	3	9
3	6	4	5	7	9	2	1	8
5	4	2	1	3	7	8	9	6
8	7	3	9	5	6	1	2	4
9	1	6	2	4	8	5	7	3

Sudoku, puzzle 7

5	6	2	3	7	9	1	4	8
3	9	8	6	4	1	7	5	2
7	4	1	2	5	8	3	6	9
4	8	3	7	2	6	9	1	5
6	1	9	8	3	5	4	2	7
2	5	7	9	1	4	6	8	3
9	3	6	4	8	2	5	7	1
1	2	4	5	9	7	8	3	6
8	7	5	1	6	3	2	9	4

Sudoku, puzzle 8

4	7	8	9	5	2	3	1	6
6	3	9	4	1	8	5	7	2
2	1	5	6	7	3	8	9	4
3	4	1	8	6	7	9	2	5
5	8	7	3	2	9	6	4	1
9	2	6	5	4	1	7	3	8
1	5	3	7	8	4	2	6	9
7	6	4	2	9	5	1	8	3
8	9	2	1	3	6	4	5	7

Sudoku, puzzle 9

6	4	8	1	9	2	7	3	5
9	3	1	4	7	5	6	2	8
5	2	7	3	8	6	1	4	9
2	8	3	7	4	1	9	5	6
4	1	9	6	5	8	2	7	3
7	6	5	2	3	9	4	8	1
3	9	6	8	2	7	5	1	4
8	5	2	9	1	4	3	6	7
1	7	4	5	6	3	8	9	2

Sudoku, puzzle 10

4	1	9	7	5	2	3	6	8
6	7	8	9	1	3	5	4	2
5	2	3	8	6	4	1	7	9
1	4	6	2	7	8	9	5	3
8	9	2	5	3	6	4	1	7
3	5	7	4	9	1	2	8	6
7	3	4	6	2	5	8	9	1
2	6	5	1	8	9	7	3	4
9	8	1	3	4	7	6	2	5

BRAIN TRAINING the JAPANESE WAY

Sudoku, puzzle 11

3	6	4	8	2	7	1	5	9						
8	7	1	5	9	3	2	4	6						
5	9	2	4	6	1	7	3	8						
1	4	9	6	7	5	3	8	2						
2	5	3	1	8	9	4	6	7						
6	8	7	3	4	2	5	9	1						
9	2	5	7	3	8	6	1	4	8	5	9	2	3	7
7	3	6	9	1	4	8	2	5	6	3	7	1	4	9
4	1	8	2	5	6	9	7	3	2	4	1	5	6	8
						2	3	1	9	8	4	7	5	6
						7	4	8	5	6	3	9	2	1
						5	6	9	7	1	2	4	8	3
						4	9	6	1	2	8	3	7	5
						3	5	7	4	9	6	8	1	2
						1	8	2	3	7	5	6	9	4

Sudoku, puzzle 12

			9	1	6	2	3	5	8	4	7			
			5	7	4	1	8	6	2	9	3			
			8	3	2	4	9	7	6	1	5			
1	8	3	6	5	7	9	4	2	3	8	1	7	5	6
2	6	9	3	4	1	5	7	8	9	2	6	4	1	3
4	5	7	2	8	9	6	1	3	7	5	4	8	9	2
6	1	2	7	9	8	3	5	4	1	6	2	9	7	8
8	3	4	1	2	5	7	6	9	4	3	8	5	2	1
7	9	5	4	6	3	8	2	1	5	7	9	6	3	4
9	7	8	5	1	4	2	3	6	8	9	7	1	4	5
5	2	1	9	3	6	4	8	7	2	1	5	3	6	9
3	4	6	8	7	2	1	9	5	6	4	3	2	8	7
			6	8	1	9	7	2	3	5	4			
			2	5	9	6	4	3	7	8	1			
			3	4	7	5	1	8	9	2	6			

Hitori, puzzle 1

5	4	5	1	4	3	2
6	6	3	7	2	5	4
2	1	7	3	6	7	6
4	2	6	7	1	5	5
1	3	1	6	4	4	7
4	7	1	2	6	2	5
7	2	5	2	4	2	1

Hitori, puzzle 2

5	4	5	6	5	2	7
1	1	2	7	6	4	3
6	7	6	2	6	5	7
3	3	4	1	2	3	5
2	5	7	3	7	1	7
3	2	5	4	1	4	6
7	1	7	5	7	6	4

Hitori, puzzle 3

3	2	4	1	1	4	4
1	3	7	2	4	5	6
3	7	1	4	1	3	1
7	3	4	6	3	5	2
4	5	1	2	6	7	7
3	6	3	7	6	1	4
4	1	2	5	7	3	3

Hitori, puzzle 4

2	2	3	4	6	4	1
7	5	2	1	2	3	4
6	1	4	1	7	1	3
1	3	2	5	4	7	4
4	7	5	6	3	2	2
5	2	2	3	6	6	4
4	7	6	7	5	2	1

Hitori, puzzle 5

1	4	8	2	5	7	7	6
6	6	2	1	7	5	4	8
3	6	2	7	2	2	2	4
8	2	7	1	3	5	6	8
2	5	3	6	4	3	7	1
8	8	1	8	6	8	5	8
8	1	3	5	4	6	7	2
7	2	6	3	8	1	2	5

Hitori, puzzle 6

3	6	4	2	5	1	7	1
6	2	8	8	7	3	1	4
3	1	5	8	2	8	6	8
7	8	3	6	6	4	6	2
4	8	1	8	3	8	5	8
8	3	3	1	6	2	6	5
2	5	6	4	1	7	8	7
1	1	7	5	7	6	4	4

BRAIN TRAINING the JAPANESE WAY

Hitori, puzzle 7

5	2	7	4	7	8	7	6
7	3	1	3	2	3	8	3
4	7	2	5	8	6	1	2
1	1	5	2	6	7	3	7
6	1	8	7	8	5	4	8
3	2	6	2	4	1	7	1
6	4	8	1	8	7	5	2
8	5	4	2	1	2	6	2

Hitori, puzzle 8

6	4	8	7	3	2	3	5
7	2	1	4	1	6	5	1
8	4	3	2	7	5	7	6
1	6	7	6	4	8	2	8
7	4	3	1	2	3	7	6
2	5	4	5	8	1	6	1
5	1	3	3	5	4	7	2
4	8	2	8	6	3	1	3

Hitori, puzzle 9

10	9	1	9	6	9	8	9	2	9
3	6	5	2	5	1	5	7	10	4
7	1	4	8	5	5	6	9	9	2
3	4	9	10	8	10	2	6	1	5
1	2	5	6	5	8	7	5	4	10
2	4	8	3	7	3	3	10	3	6
9	7	3	4	2	6	2	5	8	10
10	9	7	9	3	9	4	8	5	10
5	8	3	1	2	7	10	4	10	2
10	3	10	7	9	2	1	8	6	1

Hitori, puzzle 10

6	1	6	7	9	7	4	7	5	7
9	9	1	2	3	8	6	5	9	10
3	2	10	4	10	9	9	10	6	7
9	7	8	2	10	3	1	3	4	6
7	6	5	10	5	1	9	2	10	8
10	4	7	2	8	6	3	6	1	9
6	8	6	3	10	5	9	4	10	8
10	4	2	9	6	10	5	3	7	1
8	9	6	5	2	4	2	1	2	3
4	5	4	6	7	10	7	3	8	3

Hitori, puzzle 11

11	14	8	2	12	5	13	7	13	15	13	15	9	10	4	16	1
13	9	7	17	10	8	2	5	12	5	11	4	15	1	6	1	16
6	13	6	17	5	14	15	9	11	12	16	3	7	8	11	10	1
1	9	16	10	16	17	14	17	4	16	4	12	8	17	7	17	2
11	3	14	17	2	11	15	6	10	11	8	11	4	16	1	12	9
8	15	2	4	6	1	12	10	9	7	4	14	5	14	13	9	2
9	2	5	15	3	15	1	15	6	15	2	14	17	12	4	7	10
14	17	9	5	6	2	12	12	9	13	4	8	11	8	3	4	7
10	2	12	14	13	3	14	1	7	6	7	5	17	11	9	2	9
2	7	10	16	17	8	11	8	3	10	15	10	2	13	8	4	5
12	2	15	6	11	10	4	16	14	8	7	1	17	3	4	11	13
15	8	5	11	15	12	9	4	1	4	10	4	6	17	12	5	12
14	1	16	1	8	6	4	4	14	4	7	9	12	15	12	11	3
17	11	5	3	15	6	10	13	1	2	14	7	12	4	8	6	8
16	12	13	17	9	4	6	4	5	17	1	6	14	7	10	3	3
11	5	11	7	14	13	10	12	16	3	9	3	16	2	1	17	6
4	12	17	8	7	8	16	6	15	9	1	2	13	5	5	14	3

Hitori, puzzle 12

5	8	10	17	2	14	15	11	15	9	3	6	7	1	13	1	12
9	5	9	15	9	13	6	13	1	13	4	10	12	13	11	10	16
15	6	6	3	11	2	4	12	8	10	16	17	16	5	7	7	1
13	2	4	9	4	8	3	7	5	16	4	10	1	13	3	17	2
13	4	2	17	6	3	11	1	4	16	5	16	8	14	8	7	10
17	10	1	7	1	11	16	5	13	3	3	15	2	3	16	4	13
4	15	11	17	10	17	5	1	12	6	14	15	8	15	8	3	7
8	7	5	6	9	4	2	17	2	11	5	14	2	3	12	15	13
2	3	14	16	15	9	17	1	10	1	6	8	11	7	1	5	4
8	17	5	2	7	2	3	16	8	15	8	12	2	6	2	2	13
12	14	17	13	15	16	7	10	5	1	2	3	4	7	14	8	14
8	1	6	16	13	12	15	12	2	3	9	13	17	16	3	2	11
1	5	13	17	9	17	7	8	16	14	16	4	15	12	9	6	9
10	11	12	8	13	5	14	8	6	3	1	9	9	16	4	2	15
16	16	3	16	12	15	10	4	14	2	7	11	7	9	6	13	17
10	13	12	1	16	6	3	3	11	4	17	9	14	16	15	11	2
3	4	15	16	14	1	8	1	9	1	13	2	6	2	5	2	17

BRAIN TRAINING the JAPANESE WAY

Slitherlink, puzzle 1

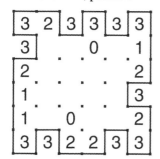

Slitherlink, puzzle 2

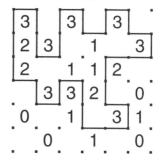

Slitherlink, puzzle 3

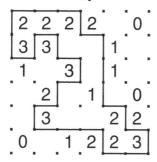

Slitherlink, puzzle 4

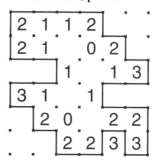

Slitherlink, puzzle 5

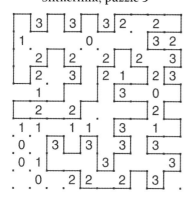

Slitherlink, puzzle 6

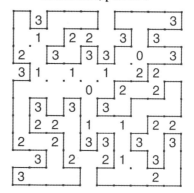

Slitherlink, puzzle 7

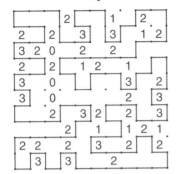

Slitherlink, puzzle 8

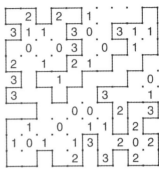

Slitherlink, puzzle 9

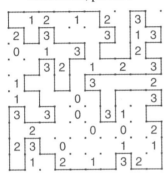

Slitherlink, puzzle 10

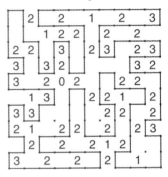

Slitherlink, puzzle 11

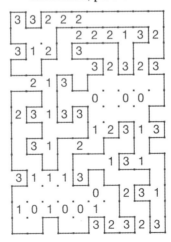

BRAIN TRAINING the JAPANESE WAY

Slitherlink, puzzle 12

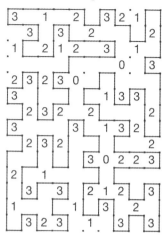

Hanjie, puzzle 1

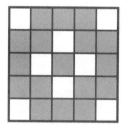

Hanjie, puzzle 2

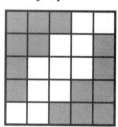

Hanjie, puzzle 3

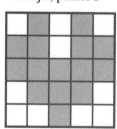

Hanjie, puzzle 4

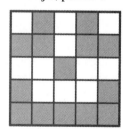

Hanjie, puzzle 5

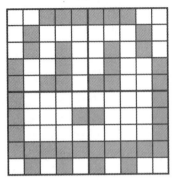

Hanjie, puzzle 6

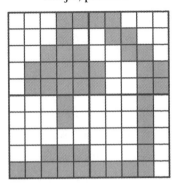

Hanjie, puzzle 7

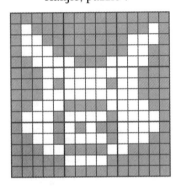

Hanjie, puzzle 8

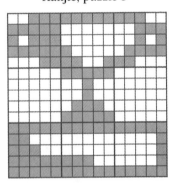

Hanjie, puzzle 9

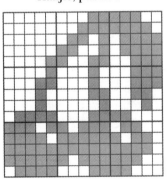

Hanjie, puzzle 10

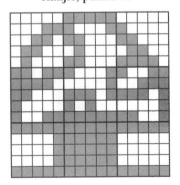

BRAIN TRAINING the JAPANESE WAY

Hanjie, puzzle 11

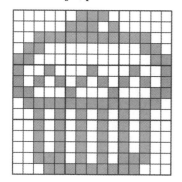

Hanjie, puzzle 12

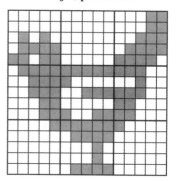

Hanjie, puzzle 13

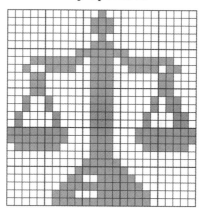

Hanjie, puzzle 14

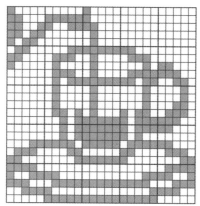

Hanjie, puzzle 15

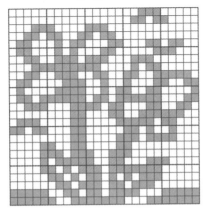

Calcudoku, puzzle 1

6+ 2	11+ 3	1	4
4	3+ 1	6+ 2	3
11+ 3	2	4	3+ 1
1	4	3	2

Calcudoku, puzzle 2

12× 3	16× 2	4× 4	1
4	1	12× 3	2
2	4	1	12× 3
3× 1	3	2	4

Calcudoku, puzzle 3

9+ 4	2× 1	2	8+ 3
1	4	3	2
8+ 2	3	4× 1	4
3	8× 2	4	1

Calcudoku, puzzle 4

144× 3	16× 1	2	4
4	3	9× 1	2
1÷ 2	4	3	1
1	2	4	3

BRAIN TRAINING the JAPANESE WAY

Calcudoku, puzzle 5

2 (6+)	3 (24+)	4 (5+)	1	5 (11+)	6
4	6	1 (4+)	5 (7+)	2	3 (22+)
6	5	3	2 (3+)	1	4
3	1 (6+)	5	4 (10+)	6	2
1	4 (6+)	2	6	3	5 (6+)
5 (7+)	2	6 (9+)	3	4	1

Calcudoku, puzzle 6

1 (5×)	5	2 (12×)	3 (144×)	6	4
4 (240×)	1	6	2	5 (15×)	3
6	3 (12×)	4	1	2 (60×)	5
5	2	3 (72×)	6	4	1
2 (8×)	4	1 (90×)	5 (60×)	3	6
3	6	5	4	1 (2×)	2

Calcudoku, puzzle 7

2 (144×)	1 (3×)	6 (2÷)	3	4 (160×)	5
6	3	1	5 (1−)	2	4
3	5 (40×)	4	6	1 (5×)	2 (12+)
4	2	3 (5+)	1	5	6
5 (16+)	6	2	4 (13+)	3	1
1	4	5 (7+)	2	6	3

Calcudoku, puzzle 8

1 (80×)	4	2 (216×)	6	3	5 (60×)
4	2 (3+)	1	5 (10×)	6	3
5	3 (33+)	6	2	1 (6×)	4
6	5	4	3	2	1
3	6	5 (4−)	1	4 (24+)	2
2 (3+)	1	3	4	5	6

Calcudoku, puzzle 9

1 (24)	2	4	5 (4)	3 (3)	6
5 (8)	6 (6)	3	1	4 (2)	2
3	1	2 (8)	6	5 (20)	4
4 (12)	3	5 (3)	2	6 (8)	1 (3)
6 (11)	5	1 (6)	4 (13)	2	3
2 (8)	4	6	3	1	5

Calcudoku, puzzle 10

2	6 (54)	3	4 (24)	1	5
5	3	1	6	2	4
6 (120)	2 (96)	4	5 (4)	3 (54)	1
4	5	2	1	6	3
1	4	6	3	5 (9)	2
3	1	5	2	4	6

Calcudoku, puzzle 11

40× 5	14+ 8	72× 6	336× 3	4	7	70× 1	2
8	6	3	4	7÷ 1	180× 2	5	7
1− 1	10× 2	4	17+ 8	7	3	6	5
2	5	15+ 8	6	3	12× 4	7÷ 7	1
7+ 6	1	7	13+ 2	5	8	32× 4	7+ 3
336× 7	17+ 3	2	5× 5	6	1	12+ 8	4
4	7	5	1	18+ 2	6	6× 3	48× 8
3	4	1	7	8	5	2	6

Calcudoku, puzzle 12

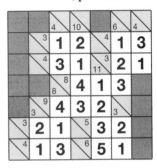

16 6	2	8	3 1	3	2 7	5	28 4
224 8	4	36 6	80 5	5 1	30 3	2	7
7	3	2	8	4	5	6 1	17 6
60 5	1	2 3	2	48 6	4	7	8
4	13 7	1	6	80 5	2	192 8	3
3	6	20 5	28 7	8	1	4	0 2
2 1	8	7	4	2	6	3	5
2	20 5	4	21 3	7	48 8	6	1

Kakuro, puzzle 1

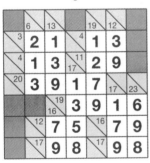

Kakuro, puzzle 2

Kakuro, puzzle 3

Kakuro, puzzle 4

BRAIN TRAINING the JAPANESE WAY

Kakuro, puzzle 5

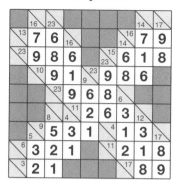

Kakuro, puzzle 6

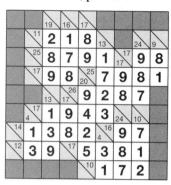

Kakuro, puzzle 7

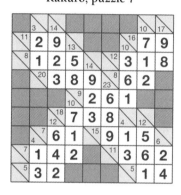

Kakuro, puzzle 8

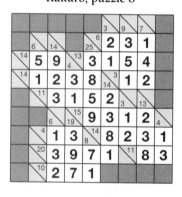

Kakuro, puzzle 9

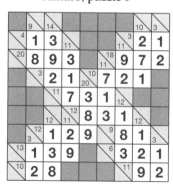

Kakuro, puzzle 10

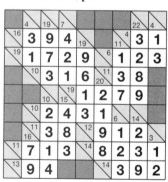

Kakuro, puzzle 11

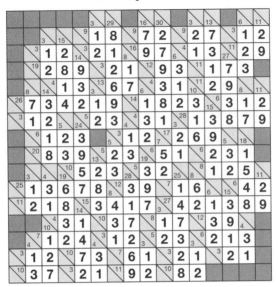

Kakuro, puzzle 12

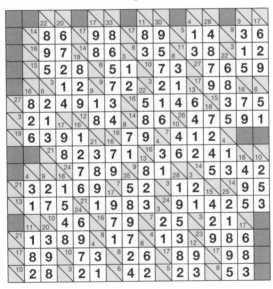

BRAIN TRAINING the JAPANESE WAY

Futoshiki, puzzle 1

4	3	1	2	5
3	5	4	1	2
5	1	2	4	3
1	2	5	3	4
2	4	3	5	1

Futoshiki, puzzle 2

1	4 > 3	5	2
3 > 2	5	4	1
5	1	2	3	4
4 < 5	1 < 2 < 3
2	3	4	1	5

Futoshiki, puzzle 3

3	1	5	2	4
1	2	4	5	3
2	5	3 < 4	1
5	4	1	3 > 2
4	3 > 2	1	5

Futoshiki, puzzle 4

1	2	3 < 4	5
4	5	2	1	3
5	3	1	2	4
3 > 1	4 < 5	2
2	4	5	3	1

Futoshiki, puzzle 5

1	2	5	6	4	3
2	3	6	5	1	4
4	6	1	3	5	2
6	4	3 > 1	2	5
5	1 < 4 > 2	3	6
3	5	2	4	6	1

Futoshiki, puzzle 6

1	4	3 < 5	6	2
3	6 > 4	2 > 1	5
5	2	6	3	4	1
6	5	1	4	2 < 3
4 > 3	2	1	5	6
2	1	5	6 > 3	4

Futoshiki, puzzle 7

1	3	5	2	4 < 6
3	5 > 4	1	6	2
6	1	2	3 < 5	4
2	4 > 1	6	3	5
5 < 6	3 < 4	2	1
4	2	6 > 5	1	3

Futoshiki, puzzle 8

1	3	6	5 > 2	4
3	2	4	6	5	1
6	5	3	4	1 < 2
4	1	5 > 2	6	3
2	6	1 < 3 < 4 < 5
5 > 4 > 2	1	3	6

Futoshiki, puzzle 9

3 > 2	6	5 > 4 > 1			

```
3 > 2   6   5 > 4 > 1
5   1 < 2   4   6   3
^               ^
6   5   3   2 > 1   4
    ^               ^
4   6   1   3   5   2
1   3   4 < 6   2   5
v
2   4 < 5   1   3   6
    ^           ^   ^
```

Futoshiki, puzzle 10

```
5   1 < 3   4   6   2
        ^
3 < 4   5   2   1   6
v
1   6   4   5   2   3
                ^   ^
2   5 < 6   1   3 < 4
^       v           ^
6   2   1   3   4   5
v       ^
4   3   2   6 > 5 > 1
```

Futoshiki, puzzle 11

```
6   3   5 < 8   2   4   7   1
    v           v           ^
4   8   6 > 5 < 7   3   1   2
3   7   1 < 2   8 > 5 > 4   6
        v           ^
5   4   2   3   1   6   8 > 7
8   5   4   7 > 6   1   2   3
                v       ^
2   1   3 < 4   5   7 > 6 < 8
                v       v
7   6   8   1   3 > 2   5 > 4
                ^       ^
1 < 2   7 > 6 > 4   8   3   5
```

Futoshiki, puzzle 12

```
6   2   5 > 4 > 3   8   1   7
v       ^   v               ^
3   6   7   2 > 1   4   5   8
    ^   ^
5   8   1   7   2   6   4 > 3
^               v           v
7   4   6 > 5   8   3 > 2   1
4   7   2 < 3   6   1   8   5
                v           v
2 < 3   8   1   5   7   6   4
                ^
8   1   3 < 6   4 < 5 < 7   2
    ^       ^   ^           ^
1   5 > 4   8   7   2   3   6
```

Shikaku, puzzle 1

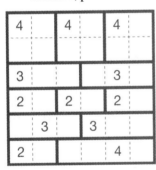

Shikaku, puzzle 2

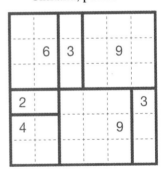

BRAIN TRAINING the JAPANESE WAY

Shikaku, puzzle 3

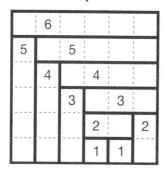

Shikaku, puzzle 4

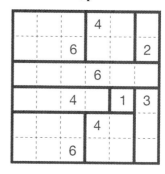

Shikaku, puzzle 5

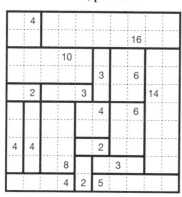

Shikaku, puzzle 6

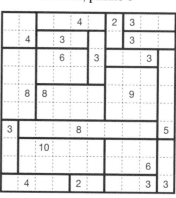

Shikaku, puzzle 7

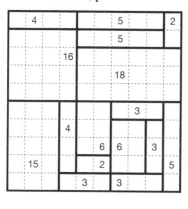

Shikaku, puzzle 8

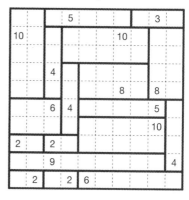

Shikaku, puzzle 9

Shikaku, puzzle 10

Shikaku, puzzle 11

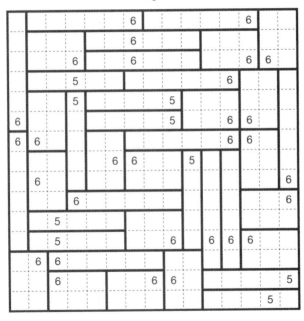

Shikaku, puzzle 12

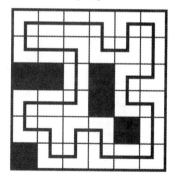

Purenrupu, puzzle 1

Purenrupu, puzzle 2

Purenrupu, puzzle 3

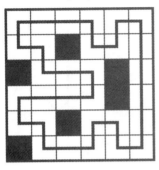

Purenrupu, puzzle 4

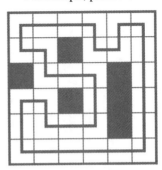

Purenrupu, puzzle 5

Purenrupu, puzzle 6

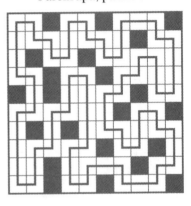

Shikaku, puzzle 7

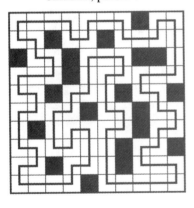

Shikaku, puzzle 8

BRAIN TRAINING the JAPANESE WAY

Shikaku, puzzle 9

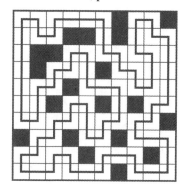

Shikaku, puzzle 10

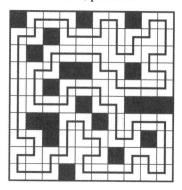

Shikaku, puzzle 11

Shikaku, puzzle 12

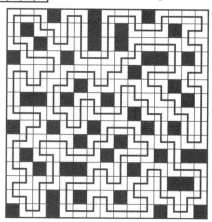

Masyu, puzzle 1

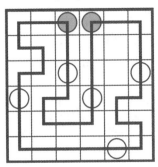

Masyu, puzzle 2

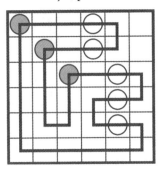

Masyu, puzzle 3

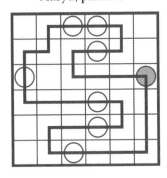

Masyu, puzzle 4

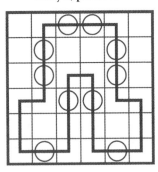

Masyu, puzzle 5

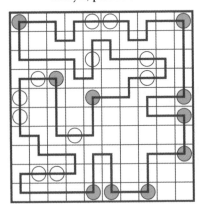

Masyu, puzzle 6

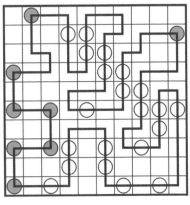

BRAIN TRAINING the JAPANESE WAY

Masyu, puzzle 7

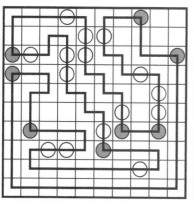

Masyu, puzzle 8

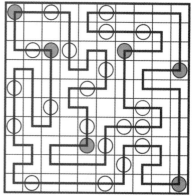

Masyu, puzzle 9

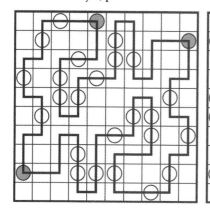

Masyu, puzzle 10

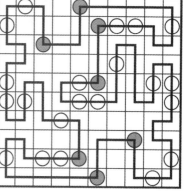

Masyu, puzzle 11

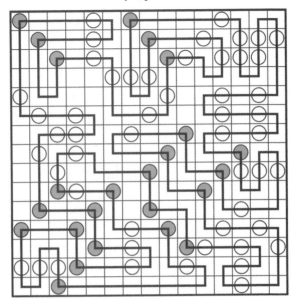

Masyu, puzzle 12

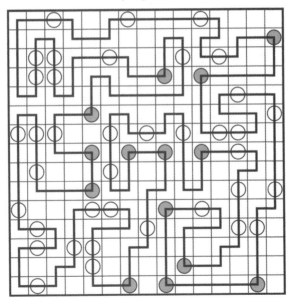

Numberlink, puzzle 1

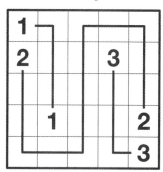

Numberlink, puzzle 2

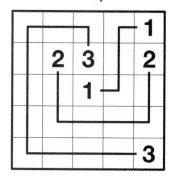

Numberlink, puzzle 3

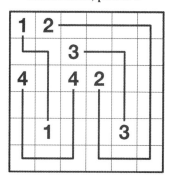

Numberlink, puzzle 4

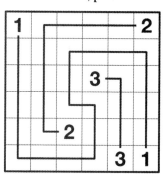

Numberlink, puzzle 5

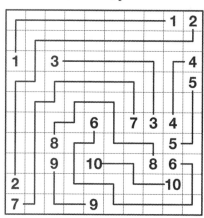

Numberlink, puzzle 6

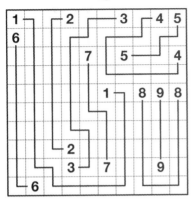

Numberlink, puzzle 7

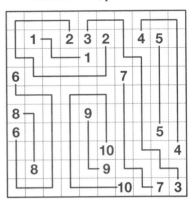

Numberlink, puzzle 8

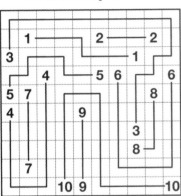

Numberlink, puzzle 9

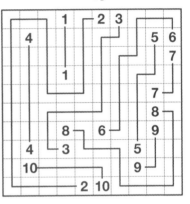

Numberlink, puzzle 10

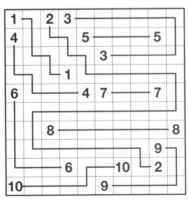

BRAIN TRAINING the JAPANESE WAY

Numberlink, puzzle 11

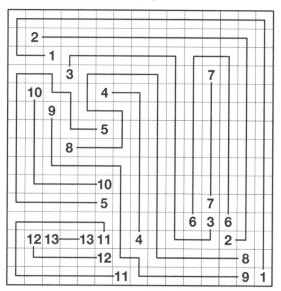

Numberlink, puzzle 12

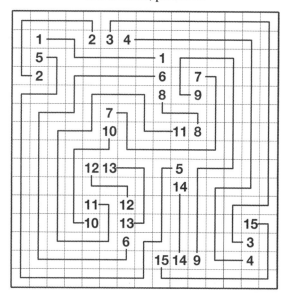

Hashi, puzzle 1

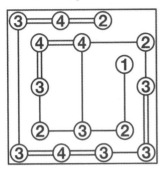

Hashi, puzzle 2

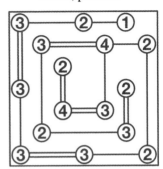

Hashi, puzzle 3

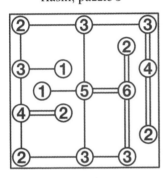

Hashi, puzzle 4

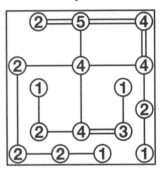

Hashi, puzzle 5

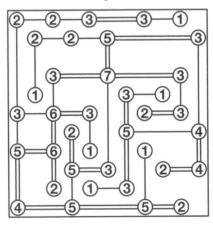

BRAIN TRAINING the JAPANESE WAY

Hashi, puzzle 6

Hashi, puzzle 7

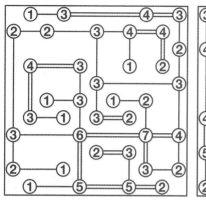
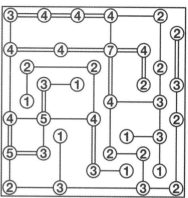

Hashi, puzzle 8

Hashi, puzzle 9

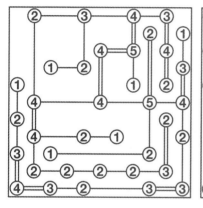
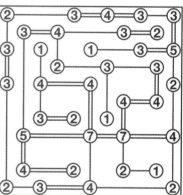

Hashi, puzzle 10

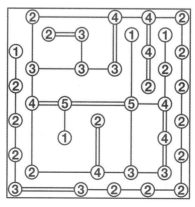

Hashi, puzzle 11

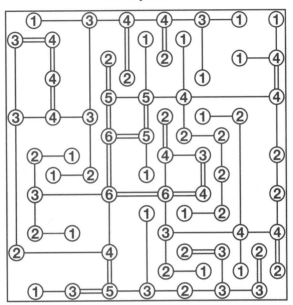

Hashi, puzzle 12

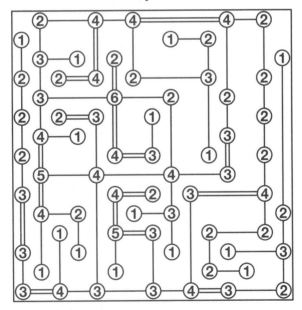

BRAIN TRAINING the JAPANESE WAY

Nurikabe, puzzle 1

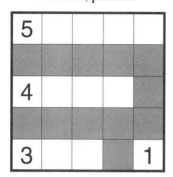

Nurikabe, puzzle 2

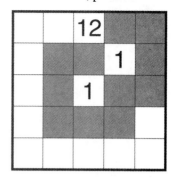

Nurikabe, puzzle 3

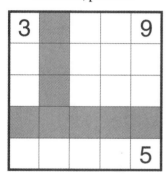

Nurikabe, puzzle 4

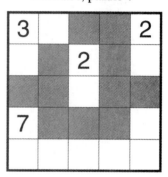

Nurikabe, puzzle 5

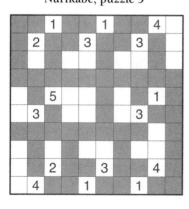

Nurikabe, puzzle 6

Nurikabe, puzzle 7

Nurikabe, puzzle 8

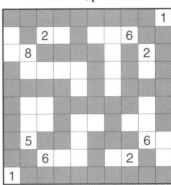

Nurikabe, puzzle 9

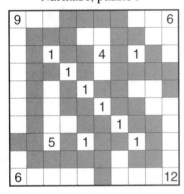

Nurikabe, puzzle 10

Nurikabe, puzzle 11

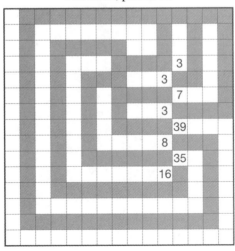

BRAIN TRAINING the JAPANESE WAY

Nurikabe, puzzle 12

Yajilin, puzzle 1

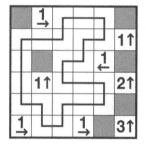

Yajilin, puzzle 2

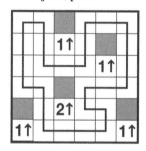

Yajilin, puzzle 3

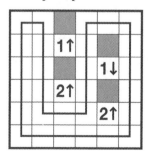

Yajilin, puzzle 4

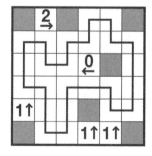

Yajilin, puzzle 5

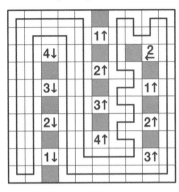

Yajilin, puzzle 6

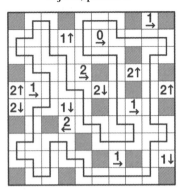

Yajilin, puzzle 7

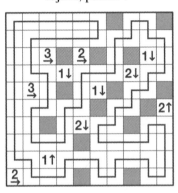

Yajilin, puzzle 8

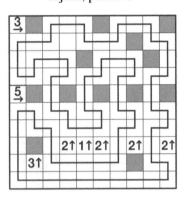

Yajilin, puzzle 9

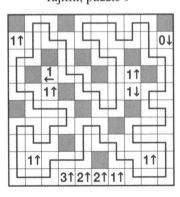

Yajilin, puzzle 10

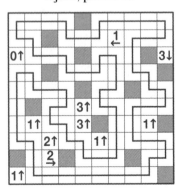

Yajilin, puzzle 11

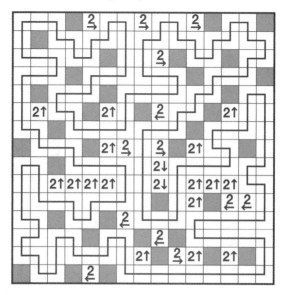

Yajilin, puzzle 12

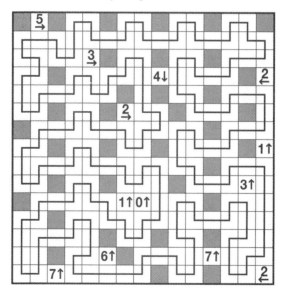

Akari, puzzle 1

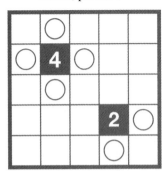

Akari, puzzle 2

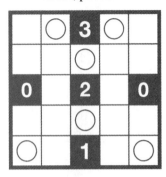

Akari, puzzle 3

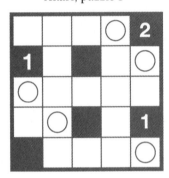

Akari, puzzle 4

Akari, puzzle 5

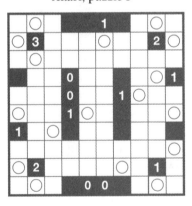

Akari, puzzle 6

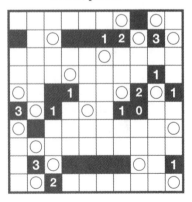

BRAIN TRAINING the JAPANESE WAY

Akari, puzzle 7

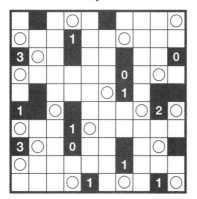

Akari, puzzle 8

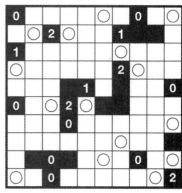

Akari, puzzle 9

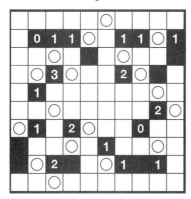

Akari, puzzle 10

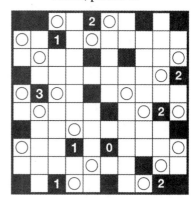

Akari, puzzle 11

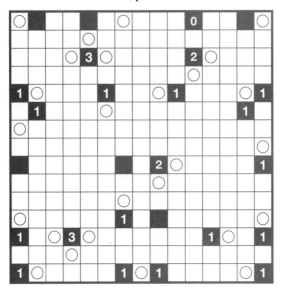

Akari, puzzle 12

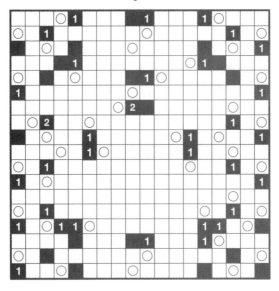

Tentai show, puzzle 1

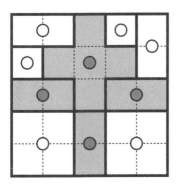

Tentai show, puzzle 2

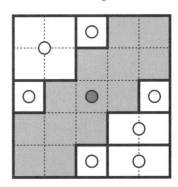

Tentai show, puzzle 3

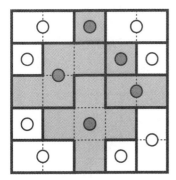

Tentai show, puzzle 4

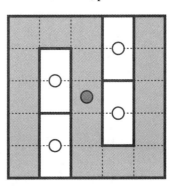

Tentai show, puzzle 5

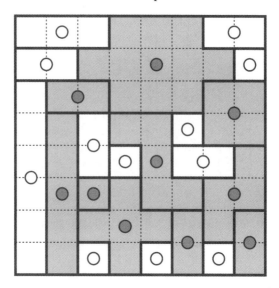

Tentai show, puzzle 6

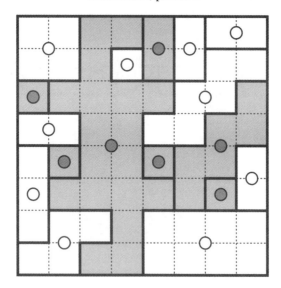

BRAIN TRAINING the JAPANESE WAY

Tentai show, puzzle 7

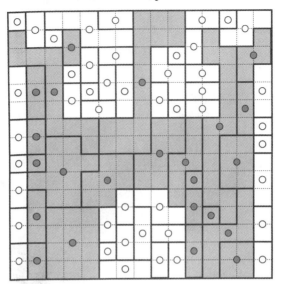

Tentai show, puzzle 8

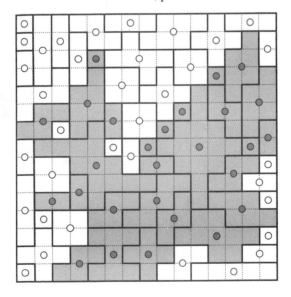

About the Author

Dr. Gareth Moore is the author of over 150 puzzle and brain-training titles for both children and adults, including *The Mammoth Book of Logical Brain Games*, *The Ordnance Survey Puzzle Book* and *Brain Games for Clever Kids*. His books have sold in excess of 5 million copies in the UK alone, and have been published in over 35 different languages. He is also the creator of online brain-training site BrainedUp.com and runs the daily puzzle site PuzzleMix.com.

Photograph by Simon Annand

BRAIN TRAINING the JAPANESE WAY